AS

English Literature
for AQA A

Tony Childs
Jackie Moore

Heinemann
Inspiring generations

Heinemann Educational Publishers
Halley Court, Jordan Hill, Oxford OX2 8EJ
Part of Harcourt Education

Heinemann is the registered trademark of
Harcourt Education Limited

© Tony Childs and Jackie Moore, 2004

First published 2004

09 08 07 06 05 04
10 9 8 7 6 5 4 3 2 1

British Library Cataloguing in Publication Data is available
from the British Library on request.

ISBN 0 435 10986 3

Typeset by TechType, Abingdon, Oxon

Printed and bound in the UK, by Bath Press

Acknowledgements
Every effort has been made to contact copyright holders of material reproduced in this book. Any
omissions will be rectified in subsequent printings if notice is given to the publishers.

Extracts from *Comedians* by Trevor Griffiths, published by Faber and Faber in 1976; Extracts from
Possession by A.S. Byatt, published by Chatto and Windus. Used by permission of The Random House
Group Limited; Extracts from *The Spire* by William Golding, published by Faber and Faber in 1965;
Extracts from *Wise Children* by Angela Carter, published by Chatto and Windus in 1991. Copyright ©
Angela Carter. Reprinted by permission of Rogers Coleridge & White Limited; Extracts from *The
Handmaid's Tale* by Margaret Atwood, published by Jonathan Cape. Used by permission of The
Random House Group Limited; Extracts from *Enduring Love* by Ian McEwan, published by Jonathan
Cape. Used by permission of The Random House Group Limited; Extracts from *Making History* by
Brian Friel, published by Faber and Faber in 1989; Extracts from *The Glass Menagerie* by Tennessee
Williams. Copyright © The University of the South 1945. Reprinted by permission of Georges
Borchardt Inc., for the estate of Tennessee Williams; Extracts from 'Under the Motorway', 'The Room
Where Everone Goes', 'The Invitation', 'The Wicked Fairy at the Manger', 'Sirensong', 'Queening it',
'Painter and Poet', 'Atlas' and 'Dying Fall' by U.A. Fanthorpe, from *Safe as Houses* published by
Peterloo Poets in 1995. Copyright © U.A. Fanthorpe 1995. Reprinted with the kind permission of the
poet; Extracts from 'Cut Grass', 'The Building', 'The Explosion', 'The Old Fools', 'Sad Steps', 'To the
Sea', 'In Sympathy with White Major', 'Vers de Société', 'This Be the Verse', 'Show Saturday', 'The
Trees' and 'Solar' (used in full) by Philip Larkin, from *High Windows* published by Faber and Faber in
1974; Extracts from 'Mrs Icarus', 'Salome', 'Medusa', 'Mrs Quasimodo', 'Mrs Aesop', 'Demeter',
'Eurydice', 'The Devil's Wife', 'Anne Hathaway', 'Elvis's Twin Sister,' 'The Kray Sisters', 'Mrs Midas',
'Queen Herod' and 'Mrs Lazarus' by Carol Ann Duffy, from *The World's Wife* published by Picador in
1999. Copyright © Carol Ann Dufy 1999. Reprinted with permission of Macmillan; Extract from *The
Steamie* by Tony Roper, published by Scot-Free, Hern, London 1990. Reprinted by permission of Nick
Hern Books, London.

Photographs © p140 Hulton-Getty

Contents

Introduction

This book is designed to help students following AQA Specification A in Advanced Subsidiary English Literature to work through their course. Its aim is to give you the necessary skills to deal with any of the texts you might study in your course, so that you will feel well prepared and confident when you come to take your exams. You may well have chosen to take English Literature at this level because you enjoyed it at GCSE, or simply because you love reading. This book will help you to build on your GCSE success, and to enjoy the new texts you will be studying at this stage.

This introduction is in two parts:

1   **How this book will help you in your course**

2   **The key to success: Understanding the Assessment Objectives**

How this book will help you in your course

This book is not a guide to individual set texts – after all, texts will change from time to time, and if you take the Shakespeare coursework option the play or plays will be chosen by you and your teachers. Rather, it's a guide to how to approach the texts in order to succeed.

The rest of this introduction will deal with the Assessment Objectives for the specification. It is important that you read through this section carefully before starting on the module. The Assessment Objectives not only underpin all the work in the course, but an understanding of them is also the key to gaining good marks.

The remainder of the book deals with each of the three assessment modules for the course. The book will take you through the design and content of each module, with practical advice and exercises. The work you are asked to do will be tailored to the type of assessment involved in the module, which might be external assessment, either open or closed book, or coursework. There will also be examples of the sorts of questions and activities which will be used to test each module as part of the examination.

Finally you will find a Glossary for the book, on pages 187–91.

The key to success: Understanding the Assessment Objectives

Here are the Assessment Objectives for AS English Literature:

The examination will assess a candidate's ability to:
AO1   communicate clearly the knowledge, understanding and insight appropriate to literary study, using appropriate terminology and accurate and coherent written expression
AO2i   respond with knowledge and understanding to literary texts of different types and periods
AO3   show detailed understanding of the ways in which writers' choices of form, structure and language shape meanings
AO4   articulate independent opinions and judgements, informed by different interpretations of literary texts by other readers
AO5i   show understanding of the **contexts** in which literary texts are written and understood

The Assessment Objectives define the literary skills which you have to show in the course. It is vital to understand that they have different numbers of marks in different modules. For example, in Module 3, which is the Pre and Post 1900 Drama and Poetry module, the 40 marks available are divided like this:

AO1   5 marks
AO2i   5 marks
AO3   5 marks
AO4   10 marks
AO5i   15 marks.

In this module, you have to choose a twentieth-century text and a pre-twentieth-century text. On the pre-twentieth-century text, you will be assessed on AO5i, but not on AO4. For the twentieth-century text, it's the other way round – AO4 (interpretations), and not AO5i (contexts).

So the marks depend on the Assessment Objectives, and the marks vary in the different modules, and sometimes in the different sections too. That's why there are boxes at the beginning of each of the three modules to show you exactly which Assessment Objectives count in that module and how many marks each one carries.

What the Assessment Objectives mean

Assessment Objective 1

> **AO1: communicate clearly the knowledge, understanding and insight appropriate to literary study, using appropriate terminology and accurate and coherent written expression**

This means that you have to be able to do three things:

- Construct clear and logical arguments. This is an important part of communicating *clearly* and being *coherent*. It means that whatever task you undertake in the course, it's important to sequence your response effectively – which means planning it carefully.

- Acquire appropriate literary terminology, so that you can express your opinions about literary texts precisely and clearly. There will be a lot of terms you already know, but you'll come across more during the course which you need to understand to use effectively in your writing. The Glossary at the end of the book might be useful for you to refer to, although it doesn't include every literary term you might come across.

- Make sure that what you write is legible, and that spelling, grammar and punctuation are accurate, so that your meaning is clear.

This Assessment Objective is tested in every module, so it's very important.

Assessment Objective 2i

> **AO2i: respond with knowledge and understanding to literary texts of different types and periods**

There are three things to think about here.

First, you have to show knowledge. AO1 includes the way you communicate that knowledge and develop your argument, but that is only valid if it's supported by evidence from the text. Details from the text you're writing about, quotations from it, echoes of it, would all demonstrate your knowledge. With texts that you're studying for the written papers, you'll need to be very familiar with them when you go into the exam. For Modules 2 and 3 you *can* take the texts into the exam with you, but just to look at passages which might be referred to in exam questions. You will still need to be as familiar with the texts as you are for those in Module 1, which you can't take into the exam.

Understanding has to be shown too. This will be revealed by the way you write about the ideas in the text – your understanding of the writer's ideas and concerns, and your own ideas about them.

'Different types and periods' is covered by the specifications for AS level which must meet these requirements:

- at least four texts must be studied

- poetry must be studied

- prose must be studied

- drama must be studied

- a play by Shakespeare must be studied

- one text other than Shakespeare, published before 1900, must be studied.

The texts you have to choose from in Modules 1, 2 and 3 meet this part of the objective.

Assessment Objective 3

> **AO3: detailed understanding of the ways in which writers' choices of form, structure and language shape meanings**

This Assessment Objective deals with how the writers of the texts work. What methods do they use to enable them to express their ideas and meanings? How effective are the methods they have chosen? Here's a breakdown of what this Assessment Objective means in detail.

Meanings

The important thing in this Assessment Objective is the relationship between means and purposes – not just the methods the writers choose to use, but why they use them, the effects they're trying to create in the reader's mind and why. It's worth noticing, though, that the word 'meanings' in the Assessment Objective is plural. A particular use of form, or structure, or language might create several possible meanings, not just one.

Writers' choices

In the questions which test this objective, it is important to keep the writer at the centre of your discussion. The writer of any piece of literature makes choices all the time about which words to use, in what order, and so on. You do this yourself, with anything you write. You need to be aware, for example, if you are studying poetry, of the verse form the writer is using, the patterns and the characteristics of the language and why the writer has made these choices.

Form

In each of the three **genres** defined by the specification, writers will have made choices of form. Here are some examples of the sort of things you might be thinking about.

In prose, the writer's first decision was probably whether to write a novel or a short story. The writer might have chosen to write in the first person or the third, or a mixture, and might have used different types of prose within the text, such as diaries or letters. The book might fall into a recognisable genre, an allegory or a horror story, and therefore the form chosen is likely to be the standard form for this type of novel. The book might be divided into chapters, or it might be continuous prose; there might be an **epilogue**. You need consider the effect of these choices and why the writer made them.

A poet may have chosen to write in verses or **stanzas**. There might be a strict rhyme scheme, perhaps in a traditional form such as a sonnet, or blank verse, or free verse. There might be a definite rhythm, which is repeated throughout the poem, or it might vary. You need to consider why the poet might have chosen to vary the rhythm and the effect it has.

With drama, you might be looking at verse drama, or prose **dialogue**. Shakespeare, for instance, wrote his plays mostly in verse, but used prose as well, and you can consider why he chose to have particular passages in prose rather than verse. Is the play you're looking at divided into Acts and Scenes? What effect does this have?

Structure

The novel or story being studied might be written chronologically or might employ time shifts, such as flashbacks. If these occur in a systematic way, you can consider what patterns are there and the effect they have on the reader. It may be important to the novelist to reveal things at a certain point, or to set certain events or ideas against each other. Some other structural questions might be: Are the chapters organised in a particular way? Do they begin or end in a way which forms a pattern? Are there passages or chapters which don't advance the plot but give information vital for the reader? Do they form a pattern?

Structure, as we've seen, is about beginnings, middles and ends – the sequence of things, why they're in the order they're in, and so on. In poetry, the structure might be shown through the way the verses or stanzas are presented – there might be a logical progression of thought, for instance, with each verse or stanza moving the thought on, or offering a different perspective on the subject of the poem. How does the poem end? With a concluding thought, a universal thought, a change of mood? How has the poem prepared the reader for this ending? When you've read several poems by the same poet, as you will in Module 3, you might start to see uses of structures which are characteristic of the poet.

Some of the ideas about the structure of prose and poetry apply to drama, too – why Acts and Scenes begin and end in the way they do, and why they're ordered in the way they are. For instance, in *Antony and Cleopatra* the early scenes alternate between Rome and Egypt. Shakespeare has clearly made this choice so that the audience starts to compare the qualities of the two places, and the differences between them. The audience could be offered another angle on one of the dramatist's ideas in a sub-plot – for instance, the Gloucester plot in *King Lear* forms a parallel story about family relationships and blindness. This is a structural device.

Language

First- and third-person narratives are defined by language – the use of 'I' and 'my', for instance. If the author's voice appears in the text, how is this presented through language? In the same way, writers may choose to vary tense for a particular effect – a sudden switch from past to present to produce a feeling of immediacy is an obvious example.

All sorts of patterns of words and **imagery** might appear in a novel. 'Poetic' language isn't just used in poetry, of course – imagery, for instance, can be used effectively in prose and drama. It is likely that there will be more language devices concentrated together in poetry, though. When people refer to 'poetic' prose, this is what they mean – there are a lot of devices, and the language is heightened. Of course, the reverse can also be true – a poet might choose to use very plain, simple language in a poem, or in part of a poem, to create a particular effect.

There are a number of devices which you find most often in poetry. You need to know the terms for them, and what they mean, to meet Assessment Objective 1, but for Assessment Objective 3 you need to be able to write about how they work, and why poets choose to use them. Just as in prose, it's patterns of language use you need to look for, too, either in a particular poem or in a poet's work.

In some ways the study of the language of drama is no different to that of poetry and prose – you need to consider whether plain language or heightened language is used, formal or informal **register**, and so on, and the writer's reasons for these choices. Drama is written to be performed, though, rather than read, so the audience will only hear the words once. In order to create realistic characters on stage, the playwright will choose language which creates particular and individual characters. The language may try to capture the words and rhythms of ordinary daily speech too, according to the content or setting of the play.

Example of this Assessment Objective 'in action'

For Assessment Objective 3 it's important to consider how these elements might work together, and that you're looking at them to see how they 'shape meanings'.

Here's an example of form, structure and language working together to express meanings, from *Hamlet*, Act 4 Scene 7:

> QUEEN GERTRUDE   There is a willow grows aslant a brook,
> That shows his hoar leaves in the glassy stream;
> There with fantastic garlands did she come,
> Of crow-flowers, nettles, daisies, and long purples,
> That liberal shepherds give a grosser name,
> But our cold maids do dead men's fingers call them:
> There, on the pendent boughs her coronet weeds
> Clambering to hang, an envious sliver broke,
> When down her weedy trophies and herself
> Fell in the weeping brook. Her clothes spread wide,
> And, mermaid-like, awhile they bore her up;
> Which time she chanted snatches of old tunes,
> As one incapable of her own distress,
> Or like a creature native and indu'd
> Unto that element; but long it could not be
> Till that her garments, heavy with their drink,
> Pull'd the poor wretch from her melodious lay
> To muddy death.
>
> LAERTES   Alas! then, she is drown'd?
> QUEEN GERTRUDE   Drown'd, drown'd.
> LAERTES   Too much of water hast thou, poor Ophelia,
> And therefore I forbid my tears; . . .

In this passage, Gertrude is describing the death of Ophelia. Shakespeare has made a series of interesting choices of form, language and structure here for the audience to interpret. The language is lyrical, heightened with words such as 'pendent' and 'coronet', and the brook personified as 'weeping', adding to the elegiac, grief-stricken tone. It's also full of sexual allusions, particularly in the choices of the flowers, such as the 'long purples'. Interestingly, this is not at all typical of Gertrude in the play. Although her sexual behaviour is at the heart of the problem, she hasn't spoken in such a suggestive way before, and her speech has been straightforward, not like this at all. This change in the pattern of her language may suggest that the writer is shaping some particular meanings here.

The interesting feature of form comes at the end of her speech. Laertes asks, 'Alas! then, she is drown'd?', which seems a pretty obvious conclusion; but it allows Gertrude to repeat, 'Drown'd, drown'd', the repetition in itself creating an emotional underscoring. The line is incomplete, however; both syllables have to be stressed, which is arresting in itself, and then there's a gap of eight syllables before the next line. What happens in this gap? The audience is looking, presumably, at the silent, sorrowing Queen.

This can be seen as a key moment in the structure of the play. The positioning of Gertrude's speech here helps to cancel out the memory of her earlier lasciviousness and betrayal, of her son as well as her first husband, and her unfeeling behaviour towards both of them, so that when she dies at the end of the play a range of responses may be elicited from the audience. Her death accentuates the treachery of Claudius and the sense of Hamlet's loss. The tragedy of her own death (which we are much more likely to view as tragic after the Ophelia death speech) is an important factor in the whole tragic effect of the play's ending. Shakespeare has used form, language and structure together to shape meaning, and to influence the audience's response.

Assessment Objective 4

> **AO4: articulate independent opinions and judgements, informed by different interpretations of literary texts by other readers**

There are a number of things to consider here, which affect the way you need to think about your texts, and, of course, how you'll be tested on them. There are two parts to this objective. The first part – '*articulate independent opinions and judgements*' – is the only part tested in Modules 1 and 2. In Module 3, where it is the dominant Assessment Objective for the twentieth-century texts, the whole objective is tested. Here's a breakdown of what it means in detail.

- **'articulate independent opinions and judgements'**

Texts have different meanings for different readers – there's no single meaning which is the 'right' one. In the exam candidates will be expected to take part in genuine critical enquiry – and this means that the teachers and examiners who assess your responses will not work to a 'right' answer which they've got and you haven't. It's your overview and judgement, and the way you go about it, which will be assessed. Therefore you need to be confident enough in your knowledge and understanding of the text to be able to form a clear, personal and independent judgement about what it means to you.

- **'informed by different interpretations of literary texts by other readers'**

The central premise here is that there is no single interpretation of any literary text. Readers of texts are all different, because everybody is affected by their own experiences and background. The way we interpret texts and their meanings can depend on who we are, and the way we've come to the reading of the text.

In the same way, literary texts may be understood differently in different historical periods, and by different social groups. Texts are bound to embody the attitudes and values of their writers, who in turn may represent the attitudes and values of a particular society or social group. Texts do not, therefore, reflect an external, **objective** reality. Reality means different things for different people at different times. In a way, all books are rewritten and reinterpreted by the societies which read them.

Assessment Objective 5i

> **AO5i:** **understanding of the contexts in which literary texts are written and understood**

At AS level, this objective is only tested in Module 3, on the pre-twentieth-century texts, but it is still important to understand what it means. There are many contextual frames surrounding literary texts – that is to say, many facts and processes which have shaped the way they were written.

Here are some of the important types of relevant context:

- The context of a period or era, including significant social, historical, political and cultural processes. This applies to the period in which a text is set, or the period in which it was written, which may not be the same thing.

- The context of the work in terms of the writer's biography and/or milieu.

- The context of the work in terms of other texts, including other works by the same author. So, it might be interesting to look at the alternative ways Shakespeare's concerns are presented in different plays.

- The different contexts for a work established by its reception over time, including the recognition that works have different meanings and effects upon readers in different historical periods.

- The content of a given or specific passage in terms of the whole work from which it is taken, a part-to-whole context. So, you could look at a scene in a play in terms of the play's structure, mood and language, for example.

- The literary context, including the question of generic factors and period-specific styles. For instance, when looking at a Restoration comedy you would want to consider the stage and comedy conventions of the Restoration, and how the text conforms to them.

- The language context, including relevant and significant episodes in the use and development of literary language. This might include matters of style, such as the use of **colloquial**, **dialect** or **demotic** language.

This module carries 30% of the total marks for the AS course. The marks are divided amongst the Assessment Objectives like this:

ASSESSMENT OBJECTIVES

AO1 communicate clearly the knowledge, understanding and insight appropriate to literary study, using appropriate terminology and accurate and coherent written expression
(7% of the final AS mark; 3.5% of the final A level mark)

AO2i respond with knowledge and understanding to literary texts of different types and periods
(10% of the final AS mark; 5% of the final A level mark)

AO3 show detailed understanding of the ways in which writers' choices of form, structure and language shape meanings
(8% of the final AS mark; 4% of the final A level mark)

AO4 articulate independent opinions and judgements (the first part of this Assessment Objective).
(5% of the final AS mark; 2.5% of the final A level mark)

Content

This module meets the prose requirement for the syllabus and requires the detailed study of one modern novel. This section of the book aims to help you in this study.

Understanding your text

From a very young age, children start to gain knowledge of stories. Take, for example, the tale of the Three Little Pigs. There were three houses made of straw, wood and brick, and a wolf that huffed and puffed and blew the first two down. However, it was probably not until you were older that you would have thought about the meaning of the story and realised that it was a moral tale about the virtues of prudence, caution and wisdom.

That's the difference between knowing and understanding; you knew the plot first, and then learned to understand themes later. The word 'theme' is generally used to indicate the purposes or concerns of the writer; the deeper ideas which lie behind the plot.

ACTIVITY 1

In groups, remind yourselves of the tale of Little Red Riding Hood. First of all, work through the story, and then discuss the ideas or themes behind the plot.

As you do so, you should be asking yourself two questions:

1 What ideas are being conveyed to the readers?

2 What lessons may be learned from this tale?

ACTIVITY 2

Now remind yourself of a novel, possibly one which you read for GCSE. Under two headings 'Plot' and 'Themes', fill in details about this novel.

Understanding the difference between plot and themes is the first stage in achieving the knowledge and understanding referred to in the second Assessment Objective.

Here is an extract taken from the beginning of *The Spire*, by William Golding:

He was laughing, chin up, and shaking his head. God the Father was exploding in his face with a glory of sunlight through painted glass, a glory that moved with his movements to consume and exalt Abraham and Isaac and then God again. The tears of laughter in his eyes made additional spokes and wheels and rainbows.

Chin up, hands holding the model spire before him, eyes half-closed; joy —

'I've waited half my life for this day!'

Opposite him, the other side of the model of the cathedral on its trestle table stood the chancellor, his face dark with shadow, over ancient pallor.

'I don't know, my Lord Dean. I don't know.'

This extract describes a certain situation, and you are told:

• there is a model of a cathedral, presumably a builder's model

• two men face each other, and they are the Chancellor and the Dean

• they are opposite each other across the table, and seem to have differing attitudes and views.

But there is more going on than this, as the author lets you know about the attitudes of the two men in indirect ways, developing more ideas:

• The face of God, reflected from a stained glass window 'explodes' in the Dean's face. The verb 'explodes' foreshadows some kind of violent outcome. The reference to God being reflected in the Dean's face also foreshadows the idea that Jocelin, the Dean, will try to take on power belonging only to God when he tries to have built the 'miracle' of a spire without foundations.

• The 'laughter' and the 'joy' which the Dean expresses will be, ironically, one of the few occasions, early in the text, when Jocelin is presented as being happy.

• The two men are across the table from each other: this suggests the hostility which is just beginning, but which will cause problems later.

• You learn of the Dean's long wait for this moment; this waiting suggests an obsession which overpowers Jocelin's mental and spiritual stability later.

• You see the different moods of the two men: one is full of joy, but the other is dark, probably with anger. The building of the spire will cause even greater conflicts.

If you put these sets of ideas together, you will have gained knowledge and then understanding of aspects of the text.

What you will have picked up from this passage are hints about the characters of the two men, their opposing attitudes, and the idea that the spire is going to cause problems. It is an informative and suggestive opening to the novel, and hopefully you will be interested enough to want to read on.

The next extract is from Margaret Atwood's novel, *The Handmaid's Tale*. The narrator, Offred, is a handmaid. Her job is to produce children for a Commander and his wife who cannot have any of their own. In this extract she watches one of the other handmaids give birth:

To the left, the double doors to the dining room are folded back, and inside I can see the long table, covered with a white cloth and spread with a buffet: ham, cheese, oranges – they have oranges! – and fresh-baked breads and cakes. As for us, we'll get milk and sandwiches, on a tray, later. But they have a coffee urn, and bottles of wine, for why shouldn't the Wives get a little drunk on such a triumphant day? First they'll wait for the results, then they'll pig out. They're gathered in the sitting room on the other side of the stairway now, cheering on this Commander's Wife, the Wife of Warren. A small thin woman, she lies on the floor, in a white cotton nightgown, her greying hair spreading like mildew over the rug; they massage her tiny belly, just as if she's really about to give birth herself.

ACTIVITY 3

Read this extract, and then analyse it using the checklist below:

1 First identify what is happening in the plot or storyline.

2 Then work out the ideas behind the extract. You may consider, for example:

- what you learn about the role of handmaids

- what you learn of their status in society

- what you learn about the attitudes and behaviour of the wives.

In this way, you are achieving *'knowledge and understanding'* of the writer's ideas, which is the first part of the second Assessment Objective. This knowledge and understanding also needs to demonstrate consideration of the ways in which writers present their ideas. This is the third Assessment Objective, to *'show detailed understanding of the ways in which writers' choices of form, structure and language shape meanings'*.

How writers shape meanings

One of the differences between prose and poetry lies in the language used, as prose writers often use 'everyday' language. The use of language, however, can be very similar in poetry and prose.

Writers of prose, like writers of poetry, use **figurative language** to bring words to life, to give them emphasis and impact, and to give them an extended range of meaning, as you will see in the next section.

Exploring the language of prose

In Margaret Atwood's novel *The Handmaid's Tale*, the narrator Offred describes her room:

A chair, a table, a lamp. Above, on the white ceiling, a relief ornament in the shape of a wreath, and in the centre of it a blank space, plastered over, like the place in a face where the eye has been taken out. There must have been a chandelier, once. They've removed anything you could tie a rope to.

A window, two white curtains …

In this extract, the colour white, or possibly the lack of colour suggested in 'white', is used to suggest emptiness, 'a blank space', the absence of life or vitality. But the word 'white' may also have other significances, such as:

- innocence and purity

- a christening or wedding gown

- a sheet to wrap a corpse in – a 'winding sheet'

- other significances personal to you.

So you may see that the word 'white' has gathered up many possible meanings. When these various meanings are generally agreed they are called **connotations** but, when they are personal to the reader they are called **associations**.

A little later, the colour red is introduced as the narrator catches a glimpse of herself in a mirror as she goes downstairs. She describes herself as:

> … some fairytale figure in a red cloak, descending towards a moment of carelessness that is the same as danger. A Sister, dipped in blood.

ACTIVITY 4

What do you think are the connotations of the word 'red' here?

Go on to choose another colour such as black, blue or gold, and list the different connotations and associations which occur to you.

Many words have different connotations. Here is an extract from *Wise Children* by Angela Carter, where the two sisters, still very young girls, receive gifts from their 'parent':

> Then we were all dancing, right there, in the breakfast room, and, as for us, we haven't stopped dancing yet, have we, Nora? We'll go on dancing till we drop.
>
> > Dream awhile, scheme awhile …
>
> What a joy it is to dance and sing!

ACTIVITY 5

In this novel the two girls try to search out their father. Along the way they face all sorts of difficulties as they opt for a life on stage as 'hoofers', or dancers in review shows. They mix mostly with theatrical people. What do you think the ideas of singing and dancing imply?

You might think about:

- singing as evidence of joy

- the idea of dance and evidence of patterns in movement as people dance together: might the girls find patterns in their own lives?

- the harmony and peace found in singing and dancing: might the girls find this peace for themselves?

- the energy implied by song and dance: will there be a sense of vitality in the novel, as the girls work through their lives together triumphantly?

ACTIVITY 6

Look at the words 'sea', 'fire' and 'water'. Write down the connotations and associations which these words hold for you. Then compare these with a partner.

As well as carefully choosing individual words, prose writers, like poets, use imagery to draw attention to what they are writing about, and to try to make the reader see things in a new light. The use of imagery allows links or comparisons to be made between one idea and another and may be used to achieve particular effects. Sometimes the link is obvious, but sometimes it can be unexpected or even shocking. In this way ideas can be conveyed powerfully and with impact, making the reader use his or her imagination and experience to understand what the writer is trying to say. Two types of figurative language are **similes** and **metaphors**.

Similes

Think about how you might describe a child or a friend. You might use phrases like:

- 'She is as pretty as a picture'; or

- 'He is as sweet as sugar'; or of a boxer, for example,

- 'He fought like a lion'.

All of these examples use a simile, a comparison of two things linked by the words 'as' or 'like'.

How do these comparisons work?

- 'She is as pretty as a picture' calls up a visual image. She is compared to a beautiful painting, so the image reinforces the idea of perfection. That is the point of this simile.

- 'He is as sweet as sugar' is a simile which suggests taste, the sweetness of sugar; the boy is sweet, but sugar can also be too sweet. The phrase therefore suggests that the sweetness could be a little too much.

- 'He fought like a lion' suggests qualities that we associate with lions, such as strength, power, danger, wildness, courage, fear. There is also an association with touch here, implied in the thought of those dreadful claws tearing at somebody or something.

ACTIVITY 7

Write six sentences using similes with the words 'as' or 'like'. Try to include the different senses of taste, touch, sight, sound and smell. Following the model above, try to explain the effects of the similes.

How do similes work in literary prose texts? Here is an example from William Golding's novel, *The Spire*. In the novel, the Dean wants to adorn the cathedral with a tall spire. He thinks that this will be an act of reverence to God, almost like a prayer. Looking at the model of the building, he picks up the spire and then the author writes that he:

… held the thing devoutly, like a relic …

ACTIVITY 8

Look at the simile used here: 'like a relic'. What effect does this simile have on you? You might think about:

- why the writer uses the word 'devoutly'

- the choice of the word 'relic'. Normally a relic is part of a saint's body or of his personal belongings which believers treat with reverence. Yet this is how the Dean treats the model spire. Why do you think he does this?

- whether there is a suggestion, as many critics believe, that the spire has phallic overtones. Could the energy devoted to building the spire be a replacement for sexual energy?

- what you make of the Dean's attitude here. Might you feel that his spiritual values have become a little muddled, perhaps because of his obsession?

Here is a second example from Ian McEwan's novel *Enduring Love*. One of the themes of this novel is a debate about whether we can choose our own lives and destinies, or whether it is all predetermined for us, and we have, in fact, no choice in what happens to us. Because this idea is playing on his mind, the narrator, Joe Rose, uses a simile:

'Imagine the smallest possible bit of water that can exist … . Now think of billions, trillions, of them, piled on top of each other in all directions, stretching almost to infinity. And now think of the river bed as a long shallow slide, like a winding muddy chute, that's a hundred miles long stretching to the sea …'

ACTIVITY 9

The reference to the 'chute' is vague; is it a water chute for play, or is it like those used, for example, by loggers conveying logs to the sawmill to be cut up? There are at least two possible ideas behind this simile. There is an idea of the impossibility of resisting such a powerful force; and the idea of how helpless humans would be if they tried to stop natural forces. Can you work out how these ideas can be traced here? Can you think of any other ideas? Why do you think that McEwan used the phrase '*muddy* chute'?

The similes make us ask questions about aspects of the books which are important to the authors. These questions and ideas help us to create many meanings, and to gather meanings as we read through the book. This is called a **cumulative** process.

Metaphors

A metaphor works like an indirect simile, without the words 'as' or 'like'. It is a comparison in which one thing is given the qualities of another. For example, you might say 'He stretched himself to the limit in his studies', knowing that he did not *literally* stretch himself. The image likens him to a piece of elastic, to suggest how hard the boy worked or 'stretched' himself. As in poetry, the use of metaphor is important to writers of prose texts.

You probably use metaphors in your everyday speech without realising it. If you were to describe someone as a 'wet blanket' you would not mean that literally. You would mean that the person had 'dampened' your enthusiasm just as a blanket might be used to put out a fire.

ACTIVITY 10

Now make a list of six metaphors that you use in everyday speech.

Writers use metaphors to create layers of meaning in their writing.

At the centre of his novel *Enduring Love*, the novelist Ian McEwan uses the metaphor of a balloon going up. At the beginning of the novel, the narrator Joe and his girlfriend Clarissa watch as the flight goes out of control and the men try to hold the balloon down:

… someone let go, and the balloon and its hangers-on lurched upwards another several feet … But letting go was in our nature too. Selfishness is also written on our hearts … By the time I got to my feet the balloon was fifty yards away, and one man was still dangling by his rope.

ACTIVITY 11

Study this episode to see how the writer develops ideas about human nature, (they are similar to those you saw earlier on page 8) and ask yourself these questions:

- How much control do we really have in our lives?

- What is our responsibility to others?

Here are some further examples of metaphors from the novel *Possession*, by A. S. Byatt. To understand the metaphors you need to grasp the structure of the book which may be described as a series of interfitting frames. On the outside there is you, the reader, looking in; then there is the author, controlling the narrative and manipulating the characters to suit her purposes. The next frame inwards is the modern aspect of the novel, the tale of the two modern writers in particular, who are tracing the sequence of letters and the central relationship at the heart of the book, an inner frame. This consists of the relationship between Randolph Ash and Christabel LaMotte, the Victorian writers/lovers, and at the very heart of the book there are the documents which they exchange. These different frames need to be pinned together to hold the structure of the book firm, and this is done partly by the use of two metaphors, that of the quest, and that of possession.

Even if you are not studying *Possession*, you will find this aspect interesting, because the idea of the quest and also of possession is evident in all of the set texts, whether your choice is *Enduring Love, The Handmaid's Tale, The Spire,* or *Wise Children*.

The idea of a quest has always been important in literature, from Greek and Roman times with the stories of Odysseus and Aeneas, and in the medieval period with literature such as the tales of King Arthur and his knights. In modern times there is the important idea of the quest in Tolkien's novel *The Lord of the Rings*. On the literal or realistic level, these heroes go out on a quest to find something. But the metaphorical meaning is important. The quest turns out to be a metaphor for mankind's journey through life seeking fulfilment, and an understanding of his/her moral and spiritual needs to make the most of the human situation.

In *Possession* the idea of the quest is rewritten in modern terms. However, within the inner frame of the novel, there is an extract from Christabel LaMotte's tale, *The Threshold*. Here, the quest is presented as a medieval text. A 'childe' sets out on a quest, so he asks for an old woman's help, and she replies:

… I have lived too long to care much for the outcome of one quest or another: …

Despite this, the child continues on his quest, and finds:

> ... banks of sweetly scented flowers he had never seen or dreamed of, blowing soft dust at him from their huge throats, and lit by a light neither of day nor of night, neither of sun nor of moon, neither bright nor shadowy, but the even perpetual unchanging light of that kingdom ...

ACTIVITY 12

1 The quest the child is on is very vague; what do you think he seeks to find?

2 How does the writer present his experiences? Are they realistic, or do they suggest certain things to you?

3 What are the effects of the **assonance**, such as 'sweetly scented'? And the effects of darkness and of light?

4 Why is there repetition of 'neither'?

5 With your teacher discuss the image of the quest in literature, and think about how a quest may suggest a spiritual search as well as the more practical or actual aspect.

The idea of the quest is repeated throughout all the frames and timelines of the novel *Possession*, and you will need to explore this repetition if you are studying this text. (Perhaps the best way of doing this would be to separate out the different relationships within the different timelines and note where the author makes links between them.) In the Victorian frame Randolph Ash believes that meeting Christabel has resolved his quest for love, 'I have known you were my fate'. In the modern frame, Maud Bailey and Roland Michell share a quest to trace the relationship between the Victorian lovers; but they are both loveless, and another sort of quest is fulfilled at the end of the novel after they admit their love for each other, and spend their first night together as lovers:

> In the morning, the whole world had a strange new smell. It was the smell of the aftermath, a green smell, a smell of shredded leaves and oozing resin, of crushed wood and splashed sap, a tart smell, which bore some relation to the smell of bitten apples. It was the smell of death and destruction and it smelled fresh and lively and hopeful.

This is obviously a very complex and abstract way of describing the situation when they wake up together after their first love-making.

ACTIVITY 13

There are several metaphors at work here, and here are some of ideas they raise for you to think about:

• What is the force of the reference to the bitten apples? You may need to explore the Garden of Eden myth.

• Why should there be references to 'death' and 'destruction' so soon in their relationship?

• At the same time, how can the relationship also be 'fresh' and 'hopeful'?

• How might the sense of energy in the 'oozing resin, crushed wood and splashed sap' refer to lovemaking?

• Perhaps most importantly of all, are you able to see how the idea of a quest has both spiritual and physical connotations?

If you are studying *Possession* you should explore how the image of the quest drives most characters. Working through the different frames as in the previous models, you might also explore how the image of possession, both metaphorical and real is tied in to the idea of the quest.

If you are studying one of the other novels, you may also explore these texts to track the ideas of the quest and of possession in them using the models above.

In his novel *The Spire*, William Golding also uses metaphors in an interlinking series to make the development of the novel clearer. The most important metaphor is that of the spire. However, this is not a stable or unchanging metaphor; the meanings are extended as the novel progresses. Here are just three of the different metaphors related to the spire itself; the first idea may well be the most important.

At times, the author refers to the spire as a 'tower', for example:

Then the tower stopped growing for nearly a month, …

In order to grasp this imagery fully, it would be helpful to think about the image of the Tower of Babel from the Bible, *Genesis,* XI.

Briefly, the word 'babilu' means the 'gates of God'. According to the biblical story, men built a tower from earth, attempting to reach directly to Heaven. Of course, men had no right to aspire to the level of God; so, angered, God dealt confusion to the builders; he made them all speak with different tongues so that the project came to a halt in complete chaos. These men were guilty of spiritual pride in attempting to reach God directly. This sense of spiritual pride and a wrong endeavour lies behind the ideas in *The Spire*. You will even see that the builders speak in an alien language to the church clerics.

Here is a little more detail which relates to the quotation above. Roger Mason, the master builder had just had one of his many arguments with the Dean about building the tower, because of the lack of foundations. Roger says:

'I believe you're the devil. The devil himself.'

But he dropped below the voice and the pillars were singing again; …

Here the link with the Tower of Babel becomes more explicit.

ACTIVITY 14

You can see this link in the use of language, so you might think about:

- whether Golding makes a deliberate parallel between the Dean and the devil. What effects might this have?

- why the stones of the pillars are 'singing'. You realise that this singing has replaced the sound of the choir in Church. What do you think the stones might be singing about?

If you are studying this text, you will see that the 'singing stones' become a repeated **motif** throughout the book. You should look at this pattern and work out its significance.

When Jocelin quarrels with Father Anselm over the spire, the Dean reads the other man's mind:

… the invisible thing up there is Jocelin's Folly, which will fall, and in its fall, bury and destroy the church.

Here the spire becomes an *emblem*, an image with a fixed meaning, as throughout the text the idea of spiritual pride, and the link, therefore to the Tower of Babel remains constant and ever-present.

The spire is also presented in other metaphorical ways, and again, you will need to explore the whole sequence. Here are two final examples of metaphors related to the spire. The first is taken from the episode when the master builder warns the Dean that there are no foundations to hold a spire; he throws stones down into the hole they have dug to show how wet the ground is. He grows pale, and the Dean looks down into the hole and sees:

Some form of life; that which ought not to be seen or touched, the darkness under the earth, turning, seething, coming to the boil.

ACTIVITY 15

Golding creates a quite shocking image here, which is, after all, in the middle of a cathedral. Look at how the language works, and think about these questions:

- Why are the ideas of heat and darkness stressed?

- Why are such violent verbs as 'seething' used?

- Why should such sort of life be avoided completely?

- Could the register be described as hellish?

- What might this suggest about Jocelin's plan?

- Can you now see links again with the Tower of Babel?

Finally, there is another image attached to the spire, when one of the builders cruelly taunts the impotent and crippled Pangall, with:

… the model of the spire projecting obscenely from between his legs …

It is obvious that the spire represents the penis here; in this way it becomes linked to the idea of lost innocence and depravity which Jocelin encounters as a result of his plans. The range of images is wide; and all the extended meanings add to the overall image of the spire.

These extracts and activities have shown that there are many similarities between the language of prose and the language of poetry. You will need to scrutinise the language of a novel as closely as you will look at the language of the poetry you study when you move on to Modules 2 and 3.

You will also be building up a critical vocabulary, which will help you to gain marks by using the 'appropriate terminology' mentioned in the first Assessment Objective. So far you have considered connotation, association, cumulative effect, similes, metaphors and sequencing. But remember: these terms are only meaningful when used to explain how writers achieve their meaning. Using critical terms without providing evidence from the text has no value. Always try to explain how figures of speech are used to achieve particular effects.

Varieties of prose writing

There are other ways in which language is used more specifically in the writing of novels and short stories. The following sections will cover varieties of prose writing, and structure and structural devices in order to complete work on the third Assessment Objective.

Narrative prose

All the prose you will read for this module is narrative prose, in that it narrates or tells a story. Within narrative prose there are several types of prose writing, and you may well find that your own text includes several types.

To begin this investigation, here is an extract from the beginning of the novel, *Enduring Love*, by Ian McEwan:

> The beginning is simple to mark. We were in sunlight under a turkey oak, partly protected from a strong, gusty wind. I was kneeling on the grass with a corkscrew in my hand, and Clarissa was passing me the bottle – a 1987 Daumas Gassac. This was the moment, this was the pinprick on the time map: I was stretching out my hand, and as the cool neck and the black foil touched my palm, we heard a man's shout. We turned to look across the field and saw the danger. Next thing, I was running towards it. The transformation was absolute …

On a first reading, it seems that just a few facts are given in this opening paragraph:

- The narrator, Joe, and his girlfriend, Clarissa, are having a picnic.

- It is a very windy day.

- As he is about to open the wine, they see something happening, something which is evidently dangerous.

On a second reading, however, you realise that there are other things going on, which raise a few questions:

- What exactly is it the beginning of?

- Why might the author stress that it is windy?

- What could the writer mean by his reference to the 'pinprick on the time map'?

- What danger does Joe see? Is it to himself or to somebody else?

- What does the writer mean by 'the transformation was absolute'?

In this opening paragraph, issues are raised about time, about danger, and about being drawn into someone else's business, which the writer continues to explore in the rest of the book.

ACTIVITY 16

Look at the first two paragraphs of the set text you are studying.

1 How does the writer prepare readers for what is to come?

2 Are there any clues in the text like the ones in *Enduring Love*?

Prose used emotively

A writer may use language to move the reader or to draw out a sympathetic response, as well as to inform. A. S. Byatt demonstrates this technique.

In her novel *Possession*, the writer adds a final chapter as a sort of postscript. At the end of the previous chapter, the biographers and critics have decided two things. The first is that the lock of fine blonde hair found in Randolph Ash's watch belonged to his lover, Christabel LaMotte. The second conclusion they drew was that as Ash never read Christabel's last letter, he never knew that he had a child. But, suddenly, these ideas are thrown into doubt when a man communicates gently with a little blonde girl:

> So he made her a crown, … and wove in it green fronds and trails of all colours, ivy and ferns, silvery grasses and the starry leaves of bryony, the wild clematis …
>
> 'There,' he said, crowning the little pale head, 'Full beautiful, a fairy's child.'…
>
> He took out a little pair of pocket scissors, and cut, very gently, a long lock from the buttercup-gold floss which fell about her shoulders in a great cloud.

The writer is very careful to avoid sickly sentimentality in this incident; so the child is made to be 'scornful' about a couple of his comments, and to forget the incident immediately.

ACTIVITY 17

Nevertheless, it is a moving and emotional moment. How does the writer achieve this effect? You might think about:

- the way the child is presented as something not quite human and rather fragile

- the way she is linked with nature in the plants which adorn her head

- the man's tenderness towards the child, shown in adverbs such as 'gently'

- the way in which he speaks to her.

This effective scene has been set up by A. S. Byatt's use of lyrical prose, so it is time to explore this type of prose writing.

Lyrical prose

Lyrical prose is often used to establish a positive atmosphere in literature. It is prose which is poetic in its force, using the sorts of devices which you looked at earlier in this section. In this extract from *Possession* the author uses lyrical prose to prepare for the moment of revelation which you have just considered. She prepares by setting the scene for the meeting:

> There was a meadow full of young hay, and all the summer flowers in great abundance. Blue cornflowers, scarlet poppies, gold buttercups, a veil of speedwells, an intricate carpet of daisies where the grass was shorter, … bacon and egg plant, pale milkmaids, purple heartsease, … and round this field a high bordering hedge of Queen Anne's lace and foxgloves, … It was abundant, it seemed as though it must go on shining forever. The grasses had an enamelled gloss and were connected by diamond-threads of light. The larks sang, …

ACTIVITY 18

This is delicate and musical prose, carefully put together to create the mood for the final moving moment of the book. But how are the effects created? You might think about:

• the use of all of the senses and of colour

• the use of alliteration

• the use of complex sentences to create a long-drawn-out effect

• how a feeling of security is created

• whether this luxurious garden-scene is intended to remind the reader of Paradise before the fall; a sense of perfection, without any threats.

William Golding has also used lyrical prose effectively in his novel *The Spire*. However, this is a dark novel, and the passage of lyricism stands out starkly from the otherwise tense prose of the book. The passage occurs when the Dean is dying. His mind and body are decaying, and he knows that the spire will fall:

> A scent struck him, so that he leaned against the woodstack, careless of his back, and waited while the dissolved grief welled out of his eyes. … There was a cloud of angels flashing in the sunlight, they were pink and gold and white; and they were uttering this sweet scent for joy of the light and the air. … Then, … he saw all the blue of the sky condensed to a winged sapphire, that flashed once. …
>
> 'No kingfisher will return for me.'

ACTIVITY 19

This is obviously some sort of a vision of heavenly and of natural things. But in the moment where Golding has chosen to place it, the lyrical prose becomes unbearably poignant and moving. How does it affect you? You might consider these points:

- How does the author use the senses to create the moment of vision?

- Which aspects of the vision are heavenly, and which are drawn from nature?

- There is a clever use of colour. You might begin by thinking about the connotations of the colour 'blue', for example the colour of the sky and of the heavens; the Virgin Mary's robe; the preciousness of a sapphire; the natural beauty and speed of the kingfisher.

- Perhaps most importantly, how does this vision affect your response to Jocelin?

- Do you become aware, as he does, of what the Dean has lost in chasing his other vision of the spire?

If you are studying other texts, it would be wise for you to check through for such types of emotive and lyrical prose, and explore their purposes as in the models above.

Magic realism in novels

To fully understand Angela Carter's *Wise Children* you will need to understand **magic realism**. This is a style of writing far removed from the realistic representation offered in many novels, such as *Enduring Love*. It is elaborate prose, involving strange language or sequences often drawn from the supernatural or from the world of magic. As a result, meanings may not always be obvious.

Magic realism has evolved over a considerable period of time, and part of its roots are in the Gothic style. Looking at an extract from Mary Shelley's *Frankenstein* may help to make this clear. In this extract, Frankenstein sees the creature which he has made:

It was already one in the morning; the rain pattered dismally against the panes, and my candle was nearly burnt out, when, by the glimmer of the half-extinguished light, I saw the dull yellow eye of the creature open; it breathed hard, and a convulsive motion agitated its limbs.

To achieve the Gothic effects here, the writer has used several devices:

- the time is night

- the conditions, here the weather, are disturbed

- there is a use of lurid colour to create vividness in your mind; it is not a human colour

- there is a sense of struggle

- the creature is made by Frankenstein, so it is entrapped by him. (In fact, Frankenstein the creator is also obligated to his creation, so he is entrapped as well.)

Here is an extract from *Wise Children*; it is a scene at one of the parties when fire breaks out and there is general confusion:

> So there was an orgiastic aspect to this night of disaster and all around the blazing mansion, lit by the red and flickering flames, milled the lamenting revellers in togas, kilts, tights, breeches, hooped skirts, winding sheets, mini-crinolines, like guests at a masquerade who've all gone suddenly to hell.

ACTIVITY 20

Using the example from *Frankenstein* as a model, look at the effects created in this short piece. You will be surprised how similar they are, both set at the two momentous times of birth and death. You will see that the subjects of both passages are entrapped by their situations.

You have seen bizarre and grotesque images, the use of extravagant fantasy, and in the novel these combine with everyday realism to convey the author's ideas. But what lies behind the creation of magic realism?

The style was made popular in South America by a writer called Gabriel García Márquez. He wrote at a time of great political violence by dictators, of untrue propaganda, and the threat of torture and death to any who criticised the government. Magic realism evolved as a way of writing apparently about mythology, dreams and fairy stories. This served two purposes:

- Márquez could mock the propaganda of the day by mimicking the fantasies put out by the government.

- Beneath this disguised writing, Marquez was able to criticise the government without fear of arrest.

Obviously Angela Carter did not fear arrest, but she has picked up the theme of truth. In *Wise Children* she explores the idea that there is no such thing as the truth belonging to one person. Instead, truth lies in a collection of everybody's ideas and beliefs. A second extract may help to make all of this clear. Again, the setting is at a party, and the uncle of the seventy-five year old narrator does one of his famous conjuring tricks:

'Look in my pocket, Nora.' …

'Oh, Perry!' She expelled a sigh and pulled it out.

Brown as a quail, round as an egg, sleepy as a pear. I'll never know how he got it in his pocket.

'Look in the other one, Dora.'

One each. They were twins, of course, three months old, by the look of them.

'*Oooh*, Perry!' said Nora. 'Just what I always wanted.'

Then Dora addresses the reader:

Hard to swallow, huh?

ACTIVITY 21

- What do you make of this scene?

- Could you believe that he really produces living twins from his pocket, or are you even expected to believe it?

- Might they really represent the idea of happiness and satisfaction in life?

- And, given that the babies are from South America, could there be a literary joke about the gift of magic realism to Angela Carter? Could the South American twins be Márquez' two great books, *One Hundred Years of Solitude* and *Chronicle of a Death Foretold*?

You will see in this last extract that the tone is playful and joyful; that is typical of magic realism; as is the comic ending. Not in the sense of funny, but in the sense that there is social peace and happiness at the end of a very funny book.

Satirical prose

In satirical prose, the writer aims to criticise society by ridiculing problems within it. Again, it is helpful to draw on *Wise Children* for its wicked satire on the theatrical and film worlds of Hollywood. Overleaf is an example, from a section describing the set for a film production of *A Midsummer Night's Dream*:

The wood near Athens covered an entire stage and was so thickly art-directed it came up all black in the rushes ... so they sprayed it in parts with silver paint to lighten it up. ... And clockwork birds, as well – thrushes, finches, sparrows, larks – that lifted up their wings and lowered their heads and sang out soprano, mezzo, contralto, joining in the fairy songs.

rushes are the first prints of a film quickly 'rushed' out.

But it all went wrong:

And that 'wood near Athens' was a deathtrap. A couple of bunnies were concussed by swinging dewdrops; a gnome missed his footing on a toadstool and fractured a fibula.

ACTIVITY 22

To make her point clear, Angela Carter has the narrator say:

'...it left nothing to the imagination ... It was all too literal for me. ... It's the American tragedy in a nutshell.'

- What sort of production do you think is being satirised?

- What do you think the real point of the satire might be?

- Do you think that the narrator has a fair point?

Still keeping to the theatrical theme, Angela Carter also satirises a certain type of 'great actor', when she describes Melchior Hazard, a famous actor, as he dedicates a stage to the memory of Shakespeare:

'And welcome, welcome, to all of you come together here, so many, many folk, to engage with us in the great task in hand, to ransack all the treasuries of this great industry of yours to create a glorious, an everlasting monument to the genius of that poet whose name will be reverenced as long as English is spoken ... [who] let some of that glory rub off on us old Englishmen too, as they set sail around the globe, bearing with them on that mission the tongue that Shakespeare spoke!'

When he said that, as it came rolling out, you could almost see the tongue, on a red satin cushion, under glass.

ACTIVITY 23

It might be helpful for you to watch a video clip of one or two of our 'great' actors who speak in this grand style. You could choose Laurence Olivier in *Othello* or Kenneth Branagh in *Henry V.* How does Carter make this satire so effective? You might think about:

- the use of repetition

- the complex sentences with built-in pauses for effect

- the use of the royal 'we'

- unfortunate choices of words.

Mixing prose styles

This technique is used by most writers to create various effects. In *Possession* a great many different types of prose are incorporated into the novel, including: formal and informal letters, tales, academic journals and papers, dialogue, traditional third person narrative, some Gothic melodrama and the language of the TV interview. There are also the poems which are expert imitations of Victorian poetry; to understand these, it would be wise to look at some Victorian poetry, such as Swinburne, Christina Rossetti or Emily Brontë. (Perhaps you might link the study of this novel with Victorian poetry in Module 3.) Each poem furthers the themes of the novel, about love or the quest for human knowledge and understanding of the human situation.

Here are two examples of different types of prose, the language of Gothic literature, and then the language of the TV show. In the crucial scene where Cropper decided to unearth and steal Ash's box from his grave, the Gothic tradition is drawn upon in the late-night setting:

Cropper waited until one o'clock to go out. ... 'Look,' said Hildebrand, standing in a patch of moonlight between the church and the knoll with the yew and the cedar. A huge white owl circled the church tower, ...

Above the owl, the dragon moved a little, ...

A wind was getting up. It flapped a little: one or two of the churchyard trees creaked and groaned.

ACTIVITY 24

Consider these questions:

- What effects do you think are created by the inclusion of this sort of language?

- You have already looked at elements of Gothic prose on page 17 earlier; can you pick out the Gothic elements here?

- How does language help to create a sense of melodrama?

- Can you see how the author changes the pace and mood of the book, so that she can move into satire about over-earnest biographers or collectors?

A second example of varied types of prose writing from *Possession* is that of the TV interview. Briefly, Professor Blackadder is invited to appeal for the preservation of Ash's letters in England, rather than letting the wealthy American Cropper buy them. He is hopeless at this, until Leonora Stern gives him some advice, which he listens to:

'You've got to get them by the balls, …'

He makes a vivid appeal:

'Randolph Henry Ash was one of the great love poets in our language. *Ask to Embla* is one of the great poems of true sexual passion … – we've discovered Ash's Dark Lady. It's the kind of discovery scholars dream of. The letters have got to stay in our country – they're part of our national story.'

*the *Dark Lady* was said to be the woman to whom Shakespeare wrote his sonnets, and the discovery of this caused much academic excitement.

ACTIVITY 25

Think about these questions:

- Do you recognise this sort of appeal?

- Can you think of an appeal similar in tone recently?

- What effects are created through the use of words such as sexual passion?

- How might this episode link in to the satire on biographers?

If you are not studying this text, now analyse your own set text to work through examples of various prose types using the models above.

So far, there have been considerations of various types of narrative prose writing: emotive, lyrical, magic realism and Gothic prose, satirical prose and the varied use of prose styles. You will look shortly at psychoanalytical prose.

To recap, form in the novel and types of writing within that form have been explored.

To complete the work on the third Assessment Objective, the following section will cover structure and structural devices.

Structure and structural devices

Structure is *not* the same thing as narrative sequence. 'Structure' means the ways in which the writer makes all the different elements of the book hang together or fuse into a coherent whole. Structure and structural devices are the ways in which the writer imposes unity on his/her novel.

You need to consider some of the most important ways of achieving this unity by exploring the following structural devices:

- appendices

- other addenda

- continuous narrative

- dialogue

- narrative viewpoint: first- or third-person narration, varied narrative account and the use of letters

- setting

- repetition and repetitive motifs

- handling of time: flashback and time shifts.

Appendices

Sometimes at the end of the narrative sequence of a novel, when the plot has run its course, the writer may add an appendix or some appendices. Normally the word refers to sections added on to the end of a book; some writers use appendices to create a particular effect on the structure and therefore the meanings of the whole book.

Ian McEwan attaches two appendices at the end of his novel *Enduring Love*. In the main section of this novel the reader has been offered an account of an obsessive love which one of the characters, Jed, has developed for the central character, Joe. The reader realises that Jed is mentally sick. The first appendix is a case history of patients suffering from a similar problem, de Clérambault's syndrome. The second appendix is a final letter from Jed to Joe. Both appendices are included for a specific purpose.

In the first appendix:

- The account of patients suffering from this illness may affect your response to the character Jed.

- You can now look back over the narrative and see things in a different light, so that the novel itself may be seen to change its nature and take on the form of a case history.

- There is a shift in the type of language used, as was discussed earlier in the writing of A. S. Byatt. The expert use of a medical register may persuade you that these accounts are genuine cases.

- This also creates variety for the reader.

In the second appendix, McEwan offers a final letter, to give the reader some background information:

> Letter collected from Mr J. Parry, written towards end of his third year after admittance. Original filed with patient's notes. ...

The letter concludes:

> Thank you for loving me, thank you for accepting me, thank you for recognising what I am doing for our love. Send me a new message soon, and remember – faith is joy.
>
> Jed

ACTIVITY 26

After reading through this letter, you might ask yourself some questions such as:

1 What do you think are the effects of this final letter?

2 How do you respond to Jed now? Does this affect your sympathies?

3 How do you respond to Joe now? Do you think that he may have contacted Jed? What do you think the future holds for Joe in his relationship with Jed?

4 Does Ian McEwan achieve a double-take here? Are your sympathies shifted back to Joe with the future problems he will face from Jed?

5 Do you think that in this way the events of the novel are projected beyond the actual end of the novel, as events are ongoing?

Other addenda

An addendum is simply something added on, not labelled as an appendix. There are many types, but all generally have the same purpose as you have just seen: to vary the perspectives on the novel you have just read.

The first example to look at is from the end of *The Handmaid's Tale*, in the form of historical notes from a meeting of a society interested in the history of Gilead, where the novel is set. The story Offred revealed was one of desperate courage in a cruel totalitarian society, where life was worthless for both men and women. Professor Pixieto explains the importance of the document about Gilead:

> We know that this city was a prominent way-station on what our author refers to as "The Underground Femaleroad," since dubbed by some of our historical wags "The Underground Frailroad." (*Laughter, groans.*) For this reason, our Association has taken a particular interest in it.

ACTIVITY 27

What do you think may be the effect on the reader of these notes in relation to earlier events? You need to consider:

- being able to see if there are any changes in characters' attitudes, particularly towards women. What is the Professor's attitude, and were the sacrifices worthwhile?

- being able to see things in a double perspective of past and present. Is the present much better than the past, particularly for women?

- the ways in which the author conveys the character and attitude of the speaker.

Here is a second example from *Wise Children*. After the main text is finished, the author offers a Dramatis Personae (in order of appearance). This is the list of cast and actors written up in a theatre programme. There is a list of the characters within the novel, and in the middle of this there is a 'real life' character, Lewis Carroll, and later on several real-life tribes and parts of nations.

ACTIVITY 28

What do you think are the effects of including this? You might consider:

- the fact that the book is centrally concerned with theatre and showbiz

- the fact that magic realism contains both the 'real' and the fantasy

- that showbiz people, such as the narrator, may believe that life is a stage.

Finally, is there any such device used in the text which you are studying? If so, what are the effects?

Continuous narrative

Continuous narrative is the traditional style of writing novels or short stories in which events are developed in a logical, chronological sequence. Here you may well see a character's life in an apparently realistic time sequence. Most of our nineteenth-century novelists, such as Charles Dickens, Thomas Hardy or George Eliot wrote in this way.

William Golding employs this technique memorably in *The Spire*. It takes the narrative forward, but don't be deceived into thinking it is a simple technique, as the movement can go out in different directions. Here is an example, where Jocelin sees Goody Pangall, a beautiful young woman for whom he always had a special care. However, he has realised, shockingly, that she is having an adulterous affair with Roger Mason when he heard them talking together:

> … and he knew in himself a mixture of dear love and prurience, a wet-lipped fever to know how and where and when and what. For it was as if the words … were tugging him out of security into a chaos, where the four of them performed in some unholy marriage.

ACTIVITY 29

Have a careful think about what's going on here; you need to look at the language and consider:

- the sexual register of such words as 'prurience, a wet-lipped fever'

- the 'healthy' language such as 'security', 'marriage'

- the darker register of the words 'chaos', 'unholy marriage'.

What does this tell you about Jocelin's spirituality and state of mind? Do you think that his innocence has been lost?

This language is complex, and continuous prose can be deceptive. You have seen how the forward narrative drive, the development of the plot, has moved in a different direction through the use of certain registers and of figurative language; in this way character and attitudes have been conveyed.

Dialogue

Dialogue is very important in most novels, and is a very effective method for the writer to develop ideas.

Here is a piece of dialogue from *Enduring Love*, where a police officer questions the narrator, Joe Rose, about a shooting, and possible assassination attempt on Joe's life.

One of the themes of the novel is the impossibility of seeing things clearly, of seeing what truth is, of finding an agreed viewpoint with somebody else. (Over such a disagreement, Joe's girlfriend left him):

'Let's talk about the ice creams. Your waiter says he was bringing them to the table at the time of the shooting.'

'That's not how I remember it. We started to eat them, then they were covered in blood.'

'The waiter says the blood reached as far as him. ...'

I said, 'But I remember eating a couple of spoonfuls.'

I felt a familiar disappointment. No one could agree on anything. We lived in a mist of half-shared, unreliable perception, and our sense data came warped by a prism of desire and belief, which tilted our memories too.

Here you are offered a piece of dialogue, and then some sort of explanation.

ACTIVITY 30

Think about what this extract of dialogue achieves:

- it reminds you of what has happened earlier

- it summarises accurately and briefly, the failing relationship between Joe and his girlfriend

- it gives a surprisingly clear picture of Joe's mind and his attitudes

- it also raises some key themes of the novel through Joe's explanation.

Work through this extract and see how the bullet points above may be proved, or otherwise.

Here is a second short piece of dialogue, from Margaret Atwood's novel, *The Handmaid's Tale*. Two of the handmaids, the narrator Offred and Ofglen, are taking their usual walk:

'I'd like to pass by the church,' says Ofglen, as if piously.

'All right,' I say, though I know as well as she does what she's really after.

We walk, sedately.

Atwood has passed on quite a lot of information very economically in this conversation. Think about:

- why the exchanges are so brief

- the relationship that is evident between the two women

- why Margaret Atwood uses the phrase 'as if piously'

- what this suggests about the character of Offred

- why the author offers another perspective on the dialogue by having Offred explain what she thinks is going on in Ofglen's head

- why the woman wants to pass 'by' but not to go 'in' the church.

ACTIVITY 31

Select a piece of dialogue from the text which you are studying, or use the extract below. Using the models above, analyse how the dialogue is used to convey important ideas, and discuss the style in which it is written.

This is a second extract from *The Handmaid's Tale*. Offred has gone to a night club with an officer:

'Well?' he says. 'What do you think of our little club?' …

'It's a club?' I say.

'Well, that's what we call it, among ourselves. The club.'

'I thought this sort of thing was strictly forbidden,' I say.

'Well, officially,' he says. 'But everyone's human, after all.' …

'What does that mean?'

'It means you can't cheat Nature,' he says. 'Nature demands variety, for men.'

Narrative viewpoint

Narrative viewpoint is the point of view from which the writer allows the reader to see events in the text. There are several ways of varying this, including first-person narration, third-person narration, the use of a child's viewpoint, split narrative and the use of letters.

First-person narration

This is used when the central character or one of the other characters is telling the story through his or her own eyes. Margaret Atwood uses first-person narration in her novel *The Handmaid's Tale*, where the narrative account begins and ends with Offred speaking to the reader directly:

> We slept in what had once been the gymnasium … A balcony ran around the room, for the spectators, and I thought I could smell, faintly like an afterimage, the pungent scent of sweat …

This achieves certain effects:

- the reader feels close to the person telling the story

- you build up a relationship with this character

- you recognise her language, which gives the book unity of tone.

But it is important to be aware that in those books which use first-person narration, writers often incorporate other devices to offer different viewpoints so that there is not too much use of a single viewpoint.

Writing in the first person allows the reader to see into the minds of characters as they are in the process of thinking. Sometimes this technique is known as **interior monologue**. You have just looked at an example of this. An interior monologue is often used by writers to vary viewpoints using third-person narrative.

Third-person narration

This is the standard form of many novels in which the writer is recounting the lives of the characters, from an apparently detached viewpoint. However, the technique is seldom used all the time, as this next extract from *The Spire* will show. The Dean is looking round the cathedral as the workmen have begun their alterations:

> If it were not for that Abel's pillar, he thought, I would take the important level of light to be a true dimension, and so believe that my stone ship lay aground on her side; … Facing that barricade of wood and canvas at the other end of the nave, now that the candles have gone from the side altars, I could think this was some sort of pagan temple; … Forgive me.

ACTIVITY 32

Can you see what is going on here?

- Think about the way the narration moves from 'he' to 'I'. What are the effects of this shift? Who are the people addressed?

- The reference to the stone ship means the church itself. Here the author slips in **irony**, for the Church is already well aground because of Jocelin's plans. There is a deeper irony because Jocelin can still pray to God; he can't later, as his plans develop. In this way this extract is a marker for his state of mind.

Now examine your chosen text, and decide which narrative form the writer has chosen to use. If it is the third-person form, look carefully through the book for any instances where you think that the writer has intervened to break the narrative account and led the reader into forming an opinion. Are there other techniques in use?

Varying narrative viewpoint

In *Enduring Love* there is a point where the story is told through the eyes and voice of more than one speaker. An example of this is evident in Chapter Nine. Here Joe and Clarissa, drifting apart, are about to have a serious quarrel. She arrives home tired and unwell from work:

> It would make more sense of Clarissa's return to tell it from her point of view.
> … before she has even put down her bag, he is on another tack, telling her about a conversation he's just had with an old friend in the Particle Physics Unit on Gloucester Road, and how he thinks that this friend there might wangle him an appointment with the professor. All Clarissa wants to say is, Where's my kiss? Hug me! Take care of me! But Joe is pressing on like a man who has seen no other human for a year.

ACTIVITY 33

After reading the extract through carefully, decide for yourself:

- where your sympathies lie between the two lovers and why

- what the writer might be suggesting about Joe Rose in a story about self-interest and obsession

- how effective this technique is in presenting two characters.

There is here a sort of **dramatic irony**. Therefore the reader is always in a better position than the characters themselves to understand situations.

ACTIVITY 34

Rewrite an episode from your set text through the eyes of another character. You need to consider how a character is established and defined:

- by what a character says

- by what a character does

- by noting any difference between what a character says and what a character actually does

- by noting how other characters react to this character

- by looking at the language the author uses in his account of this character: whether it is positive or negative

- by analysing the dialogue put into that character's mouth

- by analysing any interior monologue which that character engages in.

ACTIVITY 35

Using the checklist above, compile a character study from your set text. Look again at any character studies which you may have compiled earlier.

Letters

The use of letters in novels can create several effects. They may be used, for example, to vary the viewpoint in a story; to reveal character; to indicate the passage of time; to save space by avoiding lengthy narrative account; to extend themes. Here is another look at the letter which ends the novel *Enduring Love*, from one character, Jed Parry, to the narrator, Joe Rose with whom he is obsessively and dangerously in love:

Dear Joe, I was awake at dawn. ... Now you know that every day I spend here brings you one tiny step closer to that glorious light, His love, and the reason you know it now when you didn't before is because you are close enough to feel yourself turning helplessly and joyfully towards his warmth. No going back now, Joe! When you are His, you also become mine.

The context of the letter is important. Jed had attempted to have Joe murdered, and Joe finally shot him and injured him. As a result Jed is in his third year in a mental institution, three years after the novel concluded. Joe had already decided that Jed had de Clérambault's syndrome, deluded, obsessive love for another person, and immediately after the main body of the novel ends, Ian McEwan gives medical histories of people who suffer from this illness.

ACTIVITY 36

How does this letter affect you, and what purposes might it serve? You might think about these questions:

- Is the author offering more information to allow you to decide about Jed's state of mind?

- How does the letter act to show the passing of time?

- Do you wonder what might have happened to Joe in the meantime?

- Are you almost asked to write your own scenario?

- Could it be that Joe is seriously ill?

- Could it be that Jed has plotted another assassination attempt?

Whatever you decide, it is clear that the letter is pretty chilling, and that Ian McEwan has made you actively engaged in almost writing your own script. The use of letters allows you to look at things from many perspectives.

Setting

Setting is always important in establishing the structure of a novel or short story. You become familiar with the settings, especially if they are revisited throughout the book. In this way you gain an understanding of a character's relationship with the setting in which the writer places him/her.

Sometimes the setting is described vividly to develop the themes of the book. You have seen how the description of the interior of the cathedral in *The Spire* connotes ideas of hell, pages 11–12 earlier. Here is a second example from the same text. At first, the Dean surveys the countryside around from near the top of his tower. From above, it all looks harmonious as the townspeople make their way to market, and Jocelin feels full of 'joy'. But he climbs down and sees the town from another perspective:

> The earth is a huddle of noseless men grinning upward, there are gallows everywhere, the blood of childbirth never ceases to flow, nor sweat in the furrow, the brothels are down there and drunk men lie in the gutter. There is no good thing in all this circle but the great house, the ark, the refuge, …

There are a couple of rather obscure references here. The 'noseless men' is an image taken from the Reformation, when Catholic statues were defaced and their noses were indeed cut off. So this image works in a sort of shorthand, to show the lack of faith of the people. The idea of non-stop work and pain may be a reference to the fall from Paradise, when mankind's joy was replaced by constant work and pain and trouble.

ACTIVITY 37

Bearing these references in mind, what do you think are the functions of this particular account of setting? You might think about:

- the contrast between what the Dean sees from the top of the tower, and then from the ground

- how the author conveys the hardships of life, and the ways in which people live (You might consider register here.)

- what the author might be suggesting about the relationship between the church and the people (You might remember here that the cathedral is in such a mess that people won't worship there.)

- whether Jocelin has lost his innocence at this point in the novel.

So you see that when a writer establishes settings, they are usually more than a mere backdrop to events. Often they are used to remind the reader of the issues within the book. Here are two examples from A. S. Byatt's novel, *Possession*. Both are set in the same place, as first the modern couple and then the Victorians visit a place on the North Yorkshire coast called Boggle Hole. They will be compared side by side, first the moderns:

> They walked down through flowering lanes. The high hedges were thick with dog-roses, mostly a clear pink, sometimes white, with yellow-gold centres dusty with yellow pollen. These roses were intricately and thickly entwined with rampant wild honeysuckle, trailing and weaving creamy flowers among the pink and gold.

You will notice here that this is a very **sensuous** account, as many of the senses are involved, which can be worked out with ease; also there is a clear sense of 'togetherness' in the register concerned with things being entwined together. There is no dark side to this imagery, suggesting a harmony between the couple.

Then there are the Victorians:

> They had come across summer meadows and down narrow lanes between tall hedges thick with dog-roses, intricately entwined with creamy honeysuckle, a tapestry from Paradise Garden, she said, and smelling so airily sweet, …

Of course, the similarity between the two is immediately clear. However, what is the point of this repetition? The writer gave a clue at the very beginning of the book when Roland Michell is working in the London Library and finds a draft letter written by Randolph Ash. The poet, Ash, makes a reference to Vico's *Principj di Scienza Nuova*. This is a subtle clue about one of the themes of the book, for Vico, a seventeenth-century Italian philosopher, believed that history moves in a series of repeated cycles, which fall into chaos finally, and the whole process begins again. If mankind were to learn from these cycles, disaster could be avoided. This partly explains A. S. Byatt's use of repetition, as the reader wonders whether the modern lovers could learn enough from the Victorian lovers to avoid the difficulties faced by the earlier lovers.

Therefore, there are subtle differences between the two descriptions.

ACTIVITY 38

- What do you learn from this description of setting?

- Is the second as sensuous as the first?

- Why is there a reference to 'Paradise Garden'? Does it introduce a new note into the description?

- You might remember that the Victorian age held stronger views on religion and morality than the modern age: might this suggest something about the outcome of the earlier relationship? You might think about why the 'flowering' lanes of the first extract have become the 'narrow' lanes of the second extract.

Setting is used here as a sort of shorthand to develop the themes of the novel.

Setting can also be used to establish a mood, and to extend the themes. Here is a final example from *Wise Children,* when the narrator arrives in Hollywood:

Welcome to the Land of Make-Believe! ... Welcome to Dreamland.

... the residential motel of the stars, with its Olde English motif. ... All the little bungalows, half-timbered, thatched – replicas of Anne Hathaway's cottage – each one nestled under clematis, set in wee herbaceous gardens, tended with loving care by Japanese gardeners, ...

But the Forest of Arden [the motel] was a lovely, flimsy, fantastic place, where you could live in grand, two-dimensional style ...

ACTIVITY 39

What are some of the purposes behind this account of setting? You might think about:

- the mood established by the tone of the writing

- what the author thinks about this place

- the ways in which she shows her attitude through language choices

- what the themes behind this section of the novel might be.

ACTIVITY 40

Now make a list of the various settings in your text, and try to analyse their significance.

Repetition and repetitive motifs

Just as settings begin to have associations for you as you read through a novel, many writers can use repetition or repetitive motifs for the same purpose, to emphasise in shorthand the key themes of the novel or short story.

A motif is like a refrain that recurs in music, and can form a series of images or symbols which occurs throughout a text. Here are a few examples:

- In her novel *The Handmaid's Tale*, Margaret Atwood uses flowers as a motif. Each time they are described you learn something about the handmaid's state of mind. Blue irises evoke ideas of vitality and of freedom; the red tulips bring associations of death and isolation. When the handmaid has begun her relationship with Nick, the flowers are 'of high summer: daisies, black-eyed Susans, starting us on the long downward slope to fall'. This parallels the life of the handmaid herself, caught up in an unstoppable train of events.

- Angela Carter in *Wise Children* uses a crown as a motif. Here is an example, when the 'great' actor Melchior Hazard is less concerned about his guests burning to death in a fire, than losing his crown:

'Give me that crown!' he rasped, having suddenly transformed himself into Richard III. 'Give me the crown, you bastard!'

ACTIVITY 41

This crown becomes almost an accessory for the actor: what do you think this fact, and just the two lines above, suggest about his character?

Repetition can, however, become an integral aspect of the development of ideas, as in *Enduring Love*. The account of the accident which opens the novel is replayed many times from different characters' eyes, for example:

There was so much repetition that evening of the incidents, and of our perceptions, and of the very phrases and words we honed to accommodate them that one could only assume that an element of ritual was in play, that these were not only descriptions but incantations also.

ACTIVITY 42

- Ian McEwan spells out some of the purposes of repetition *for the characters themselves*. What do you think these purposes are?

- Why do you think the scene is replayed from so many different angles?

- What ideas might this constant replaying suggest?

Check through your set text to see if this technique is being used by the writer. If it is, work out the sequence of motifs, and the associations which they carry for you. Here are some examples:

- references to colours in *The Handmaid's Tale*

- references to possession and the quest in *Possession*

- references to the spire and its opposite the pit, and to singing in *The Spire*.

The handling of time

The handling of time is a tricky matter for writers of novels and short stories. It is straightforward in novels where time is realistic and follows a natural chronological sequence. But there are other ways of handling the passage of time. For example, how does a writer of other types of prose move backwards *and* forwards through time? There are two interesting ways of doing this: the use of flashbacks, and the use of time-shift.

Flashback

This is a straightforward concept, when a character reminisces about events that have happened in the past. The writer can then take us backwards in time without disturbing the flow of the narrative. Here is an example from *Wise Children* where the very elderly narrator makes love to an elderly man, Perry, at a party, near the end of the novel:

He was himself, when young; and also, while we were making love, he turned into, of all people, that blue-eyed boy who'd never known my proper name. Then who else but Irish passed briefly through the bed; fancy meeting you. There was a whiff of Trumper's Essence of Lime but not Perry, this time, instead, that Free Pole the night I caught a flea in the Ritz. And then a visit from Mr Piano Man, ... but Peregrine wasn't the only one dear man, tonight, but a kaleidoscope of faces, gestures, caresses. He was not the love of my life but all the loves of my life at once, the curtain call of my career as lover.

Try to work out the effects achieved by this flashback. You need to consider:

- how and why Angela Carter uses language to achieve particular effects, especially the language of drama

- the mood created in this passage

- how this reprise of past events might help the narrator, and the author, to achieve closure.

Time-shift

Time-shift is a similar device to flashback but it works in a slightly different way and again for different purposes. Here is another example from *Wise Children* when the speaker, an old lady, looks out of the window on her birthday:

> Cold, bright, windy, spring weather, just like the day that we were born, when the Zeppelins were falling. ... 'Remember *Brief Encounter*, how I cried buckets? Nowhere for them to meet on a station, nowadays, except in a bloody knicker shop. Their hands would have to shyly touch under cover of a pair of Union Jack boxer shorts.'

The only problem with this technique is that on first reading it can be confusing, but it is a vivid and dramatic way of including the past in a novel.

ACTIVITY 45

Consider the benefits of using this technique using the passage above, and think about:

- the dramatic effect achieved by the writer's use of language

- the economy of being able to avoid lengthy chronological narrative prose

- the development of the writer's idea.

Margaret Atwood shifts time in her novel *The Handmaid's Tale,* particularly at first in the 'night' chapters. Here is an example from VII Night, as the handmaid lies in bed after another difficult episode:

> I lie in bed, still trembling. ... I want to be with someone. ...
>
> Lying in bed, with Luke, his hand on my rounded belly. The three of us, in bed, she kicking, turning over within me. ...
>
> I'm not frightened.

ACTIVITY 46

In the 'day' chapters, Offred tells the latest part of her narrative as a handmaid in the new society. But in the 'night' chapters, and later in some parts of the 'day' chapters, the narrative moves backwards in time. These sections are populated with totally different characters from those of the new-society characters, and gradually, as the book progresses, the past catches up with the present.

What others ways could the writer have presented this information had she not chosen to use time-shift? What shape might such a narrative have?

Now, look again at your set text and see how the writer treats past events. Perhaps there is a mixture of devices used. If so, what effect does each one have?

At this stage, it might be useful to have a recap:

ACTIVITY 47

Having covered all the areas relating to the third Assessment Objective, now try to answer these general questions about the prose style of the set text you are reading.

1 Is the style clear or complex?

2 Is the writing **subjective** or objective?

3 Is the style traditional or modern or experimental?

4 How is word order and pacing treated?

5 How is dialogue used?

6 Is there much use of figurative language? What effect does this produce?

7 Does the work contain psychological analysis?

8 Does the writer use magic realism?

9 Is the writing satirical?

10 How is the past handled?

11 What form of narrative account is used?

You should now be able to respond fully to the three questions which relate to the first three Assessment Objectives:

• What ideas is the writer trying to convey to his readers?

• What is the experience or experiences which the writer is trying to convey?

• How is he/she trying to convey these ideas and experiences?

The final section of this module looks at the requirements of Assessment Objective 4. At this stage in your studies, the primary text is the most important thing. You will not be expected to spend too much study time reading 'secondary' texts, that is, critical texts that discuss your chosen novel, books of literary theory, or books which consider different readings of your text.

> **AO4: articulate independent opinions and judgements**

Your work on this objective should be focused on two key areas:

1 The formulation of your own independent opinion about the set text

2 The awareness that there may be **ambiguity** in the text, and that you will formulate a reading which may be personal to you.

1 *How to be an informed, independent reader*

In the exam you might be asked questions in the form: 'What do you find interesting in ... ?' or 'What is the significance of ... ?' or 'How important is ... ?'

It is important to realise that you are being asked for an opinion by your examiner. You must respond by offering an opinion or judgement. If you don't offer an opinion, or try to hedge your bets, for example, by saying 'I am not sure ... ' or 'It is not clear ... ', you will have failed to respond to the task set, and risk losing the marks to be gained under this objective. Try to be confident when you go into the exam that you do have a firm opinion about what the book means to you.

2 *Awareness of ambiguity and formulating a personal reading*

Remember that texts do not have one single meaning. The writer might have created deliberate ambiguity, or might have intended the reader to form a certain opinion. But when you, as a reader, come to the text, you bring a different set of experiences and a different set of associations to bear on your interpretation. You may well draw a different message from the text from that which the author intended.

Your interpretation is always acceptable as long as you can back it up with evidence from the text itself.

All of the texts offered on this syllabus reveal ambiguity. Here are some examples from each:

The Spire: Jocelin is presented as a sinner, guilty of spiritual pride, but is that all there is to the man? You know that he has been deceived by Alison who persuaded one of her lovers to promote him. He did not know this, and thought it was because of his own spiritual excellence. In that sense, he is a victim, and at times he is presented as such:

> 'Confusion everywhere.'
>
> After a while, Father Adam spoke again.
>
> 'You must sleep.'
>
> 'I shall never sleep again.' ...
>
> Then he moaned and rocked himself.

ACTIVITY 48

How do you respond to the Dean here? You might consider:

• why the author allows you to see Jocelin suffering like this

• how the suffering is portrayed.

Do you feel some sympathy for this man, who had not, after all, intended to do harm?

The Handmaid's Tale: is it science-fiction; a love story or a historical document? Why does Margaret Atwood keep offering the reader choices in the way the book develops? You can see this at intervals throughout the novel, for example in Chapter Seven:

If it's a story I'm telling, then I have control over the ending. …

It isn't a story I'm telling.

It's also a story I'm telling, in my head, as I go along.

Then at the ending you read:

And so I step up, into the darkness within; or else the light.

ACTIVITY 49

• Why do you think that Margaret Atwood draws attention to the fact that the novel is a literary construct?

• Might she be giving the reader choices? Or is she showing the reader how to construct prose fiction?

• Does your chosen author use any such devices as reminding you of the artificiality of the novel form?

Possession: is full of ambiguities, in the letters, the fragments, the riddles of the poems themselves, the mystery of the lock of hair, the unread letter and the child, and the complicated structure. Perhaps the author is revealing as one of her themes how complex, difficult and demanding the art of writing biography is.

Enduring Love: is it a biography; a love story; is it about 'enduring', i.e. everlasting love, or is it about 'enduring', i.e. surviving love; is it a medical casebook; a murder story?

Wise Children: is it a biography; a satire on theatre and theatrical people; a consideration of what truth is; a study of approaching old age?

The point is, of course, that all these readings are true and exist together. There will be other meanings not considered here. It is up to you to make your decision as a *personal reading* of which means most to you, and to have some preference if you are asked to give one. But you must always hold all the meanings in your head.

ACTIVITY 50

Begin by selecting an episode from your set text and work in groups to discuss any ambiguities you can find. Then show how this episode supports a particular reading.

- *A feminist reading*

During the course of this module you have looked at several examples of work which could be regarded as feminist writing by Margaret Atwood and Angela Carter.

In *The Handmaid's Tale*, Margaret Atwood can be seen exploring the lives of women who are deprived of their rights and roles in life. The next two extracts from *The Handmaid's Tale* illustrate a woman's loss of rights in the society described by Offred.

I wait, washed, brushed, fed, like a prize pig. Sometime in the eighties they invented pig balls, for pigs who were being fattened in pens … they liked to have something to think about …

I wish I had a pig ball.

and

I lie on my back, fully clothed except for the healthy white cotton underdrawers …

My red skirt is hitched up to my waist, though no higher. Below it the Commander is fucking. What he is fucking is the lower part of my body. I do not say making love, because this is not what he's doing.

ACTIVITY 51

How does Margaret Atwood reveal the low status of the female handmaid in these extracts? Look carefully at the ways in which she uses language and imagery.

The end of *Wise Children* is triumphantly feminist. You see the narrator and her twin sister, who've had tough lives as illegitimate girls earning their living as 'hoofers', or dancers, in tatty reviews celebrating life:

There was dancing and singing all along Bard Road that day and we'll go on singing and dancing until we drop in our tracks, won't we kids.

What a joy it is to dance and sing!

ACTIVITY 52

Don't you think that this is a lovely assertion of life, happiness and vitality? This is precisely why earlier in the section on 'Magic realism' you will have read that it is an essentially comic mode.

Discuss how and why singing and dancing are traditionally seen as symbols of life. Have you encountered this in any other books that you have read?

- ## A socialist or Marxist reading

These readings rest on attitudes to class structure and behaviour. You could apply a Marxist reading to William Golding's novel, *The Spire*. Obviously the novel in not a political novel, but there are satirical elements connected to Jocelin's reverence for the Holy Nail, in the sense that there is mockery of the superstitions attached to some religious beliefs or practices. Initially, Jocelin had written to the bishop asking for money. But what he got instead was a sacred relic, the Holy Nail. The building costs are rising, and there are dreadful problems because the ground won't hold foundations, but Jocelin brushes problems aside:

'For what is money after all? But far, far, oh infinitely more valuable —'

What do you make of Jocelin's attitude here? Later, it becomes clear that the Nail has obsessed him completely:

Then Father Anonymous gave It to him in a silver box, and he received It kneeling on his knees ... He said to the Nail 'Oh be quick!' ... He heard Father Anselm speak softly.

'Why shouldn't he see him as he is?'

---

* *he* is the head of the visiting churchmen who have come to assess the Dean's health.

ACTIVITY 53

- How does the author present Jocelin's instability here? Why do you think that 'It' is capitalised?

- Can you see how ludicrous the idea of this is to a Marxist, who will not have Christian beliefs?

In Activity 51 on *The Handmaid's Tale* you considered how a totalitarian society destroys individuals, and there are many examples of harshness and cruelty throughout the novel. Here is another, when a condemned man is handed over to them at a meeting for the handmaids to take part in 'Particicution'. Offred is shocked to see her friend taking part in the brutality. Her friend explains why:

'Don't be stupid. He wasn't a rapist at all, he was a political. He was one of ours. I knocked him out. Put him out of his misery. Don't you know what they're doing to him?'

ACTIVITY 54

- Do *you* realise what 'they' are doing?

- Can you see two objectives being achieved here? How does it suit the totalitarian, brutal government's needs? Consider the effects on the suppressed, depressed handmaids.

• *A psychoanalytical reading*

This type of reading is based on psychoanalysis of the subconscious mind. The novels of William Golding are open to this type of reading, and in *The Spire* the author offers a study of Jocelin's mind as he succumbs to the sin of spiritual pride and pays for it with his faith, his failures as a churchman, and with his life. The author makes this point clear. Early in the novel, the Dean becomes aware of the dangers of his plan for the building of the spire, 'I see now it'll destroy us of course.' As he is dying, this becomes obvious:

Sometimes, standing in the dim church, he would put propositions to himself, though the spire in his head prevented him from coming to a conclusion. …

'It's part of the cost, you see.'

ACTIVITY 55

- How does the author use the image of the spire here?

- What do you now know about Jocelin's state of mind, and the effects of his plans?

Other readers may well suggest that there is also a Freudian reading, that the spire represents the phallus, as you saw on pages 7 and 13 earlier, and that the passion for building the spire has replaced the priest's sexual passion.

There is also a *psychological* reading in this story of a man completely obsessed with the spire and the idea of building the spire, and that this causes frequent battles of wills with the other fathers and with the builders. Golding refers to the Dean's 'dedicated will', and makes many other such comments, as you have already seen above.

- *Several readings within a text*

Texts are open to multiple readings as you considered earlier under the heading of ambiguity. Here are some ideas about A. S. Byatt's novel, *Possession*. You have already considered some readings, such as a love story, a novel about the art of biography, an exploration of the nature of history and about the human situation in moral and spiritual terms, and there are more:

1 a romance, a tale told with super-human elements and rich imaginative detail, often drawing on other-worldly beings, and far removed from realism

2 a detective story about solving clues in a mystery about the two Victorians

3 a satire on collectors and their greed

4 feminist literature, with so many aspects of feminist writers included.

And of course, there are other genres at play here, which you will uncover as you work through this text.

ACTIVITY 56

Working in groups, discuss and compare your own interpretations or readings of the text you are studying. Be careful to base all these readings on textual evidence.

Remember there are three aspects to consider when addressing Assessment Objective 4:

1 be confident in holding and expressing an opinion or judgement

2 be aware of ambiguities of meaning, character or situation in your text

3 be able to support your reading with close textual evidence.

Summary

To conclude your work on this module, here is a summary list of questions to help you to explore your set text:

- What ideas is the writer trying to convey to the reader?

- What experience or experiences is he/she trying to convey?

- How has he/she tried to convey these ideas and experiences?

- How do I respond to the writer's ideas?

- Do I agree with what the writer is saying?

- In what ways are the ideas original, or valuable or interesting?

- Does this text appeal to me? Why or why not?

- Can I support my reading(s) of the text?

Preparing for a closed book examination

It is important to know your text very well, as it is for all types of exam. A significant difference in a closed book examination is the way in which textual evidence is handled. There are four things to bear in mind:

1 You always need to support your arguments with textual evidence.

2 You do not need to learn large chunks of text off by heart.

3 Examiners will be satisfied with short but relevant phrases for examples of style

and/or

4 Examiners will be satisfied with close echoes of the text, as long as there is a clear indication as to exactly which part of the text you are using as evidence.

Now you have worked through this first section of the book, you should have some confidence in your own abilities. You have acquired the necessary skills to handle the Assessment Objectives and to understand your chosen text. Perhaps these exercises have helped you to enjoy your work? That would be good, for it is true that the more you put into a thing, the more you get out of it.

Module ② Shakespeare

This module carries 30% of the total marks for the AS course. The marks are divided amongst the Assessment Objectives like this:

ASSESSMENT OBJECTIVES

AO1 communicate clearly the knowledge, understanding and insight appropriate to literary study, using appropriate terminology and accurate and coherent written expression
(8% of the final AS mark; 4% of the final A level mark)

AO2i respond with knowledge and understanding to a literary text
(10% of the final AS mark; 5% of the final A level mark)

AO3 show detailed understanding of the ways in which writers' choices of form, structure and language shape meanings
(7% of the final AS mark; 3.5% of the final A level mark)

AO4 articulate independent opinions and judgements.
(5% of the final AS mark; 2.5% of the final A level mark)

Approaching Shakespeare for this module

You will already have studied Shakespeare, at both Key Stage Three and GCSE. At AS level you should understand more about Shakespeare's craft, and have the chance to explore and enjoy another play. Although you might look at some critics' opinions of Shakespeare in class, it's *your* opinions that count most, both in reading the play and in writing for the exam.

There are two ways of being assessed for this module: through a written examination paper or through coursework. If you choose the exam option, you have to choose from three texts named in the specification. If you choose to do coursework, you can choose any play by Shakespeare, subject to the restrictions outlined in the section on coursework (see page 57).

Whichever assessment route you choose, the most important thing to remember is that your writing has to address the Assessment Objectives for the module. Of course, a very wide range of tasks could be set by the examination board, or by your teacher, which would test your '*knowledge and understanding*' (AO2i) of the text you've chosen. You will also have to show '*understanding of the ways in which writers' choices of form, structure and language shape meanings*' (AO3), and '*articulate independent opinions and judgements*' (AO4) grounded in the text.

The first part of this section will deal with Assessment Objectives 3 and 4 – identifying and using choices of form, structure and language, and forming independent judgements. An understanding of these issues is important to your success whichever assessment option you take.

> **AO3: detailed understanding of the ways in which writers' choices of form, structure and language shape meanings**

The first thing to say here is that with Shakespeare, as with any other writer, it's the whole objective that's being looked at; in other words, you're not interested simply in what the choices *are*, but what they *do* – how they help the writer to create meanings. There's no point in writing about **iambic pentameters** or choices of imagery, unless you're explaining why the writer has made these decisions.

Form

All of Shakespeare's plays use the iambic pentameter as the dominant verse form, even when other verse forms are employed occasionally. 'Pentameter' means that there are five beats in the line, and 'iambic' means that in each beat, or foot, there are two syllables, with the stress falling on the second syllable. That means it is a ten-syllable line, with the stress falling on syllables 2, 4, 6, 8 and 10. The **metre** of the lines can make particular words significant.

As an example of a regular iambic pentameter, here's the opening line of *Henry IV Part I*:

> So **shaken as** we **are**, so **wan** with **care**

You can see that the stresses fall naturally on the syllables marked. Here are some lines from *Romeo and Juliet*:

JULIET 'Tis but thy name that is my enemy;
Thou art thyself, though, not a Montague.
What's Montague? it is nor hand, nor foot,
Nor arm, nor face, nor any other part
Belonging to a man. O! be some other name:
What's in a name? that which we call a rose
By any other name would smell as sweet;
So Romeo would, were he not Romeo call'd,
Retain that dear perfection which he owes
Without that title. Romeo, doff thy name;   10
And for that name, which is no part of thee,
Take all myself.

ROMEO   I take thee at thy word.
Call me but love, and I'll be new baptiz'd;
Henceforth I never will be Romeo.

Listen to the stresses here, and notice how many times they fall on the word 'name' – the word is used six times, and each time it's hit by the beat. That's not all, though: stresses also fall on 'call', 'call'd', 'title', and 'baptiz'd', all of which point to the problem of names. The words 'thyself' and 'myself' are also used by Juliet, with the stress falling on 'self', and this is the heart of the matter – identity. After all, if Romeo were not a Montague, but instead Romeo Smith, there wouldn't be a problem. The point here is not that the iambic pentameters emphasise words about names, but that by doing it Shakespeare brings the problem of names and identity to the audience's attention – he's using form to shape meanings.

There's another use of form here, too. Romeo completes Juliet's line 'Take all myself' with 'I take thee at thy word'. Because the ten syllables should flow in an unbroken string, the actor playing Romeo must come in quickly with his line, to maintain it. The broken line is a stage direction, in effect. What's the purpose, though? Here, it might be at this moment that Romeo suddenly appears – Juliet hasn't known that he is present and listening to her. Surprise as well as urgency might be signalled.

Now read this extract, which is the continuation of the passage above:

> JULIET   What man art thou, that, thus bescreen'd in night,
>   So stumblest on my counsel?
>
> ROMEO   By a name
>   I know not how to tell thee who I am:
>   My name, dear saint, is hateful to myself,
>   Because it is an enemy to thee:
>   Had I it written, I would tear the word.

ACTIVITY 1

1 Count the references to 'name' in the passage above, and discuss where the rhythm falls.

2 'Self' is stressed again. Which other words are stressed that refer to identity?

3 The last word stressed in the passage is 'word'– doubly emphasised because it's at the end of the line and is followed by a full stop. What is the 'word' which Romeo would 'tear'?

Although the basic line is the iambic pentameter, it's the variations in the pentameter which often show the writer at work, manipulating the form to bring something to the audience's attention. Later on in the play, for instance, when Romeo is having to face the real difficulty of who he is, he speaks this line:

> As if that name
> Shot from the deadly level of a gun …

'Name' is stressed again, but in the next line the beginning is irregular: the first syllable, 'Shot', has to be stressed. Because the rhythm is different, it leaps to the audience's attention. Why? What meaning is the playwright trying to express? The language suggests violence, and perhaps Romeo's mental disturbance is suggested by the irregularity, too. He's disturbed, so the rhythm of the language mirrors his state of mind.

Here's a very famous speech from *Hamlet*, where the speaker is also disturbed:

HAMLET To be, or not to be: that is the question:
Whether 'tis nobler in the mind to suffer
The slings and arrows of outrageous fortune,
Or to take arms against a sea of troubles,
And by opposing end them? To die: to sleep;
No more; and, by a sleep to say we end
The heart-ache and the thousand natural shocks
That flesh is heir to, 'tis a consummation
Devoutly to be wish'd. To die, to sleep;
To sleep: perchance to dream: ay, there's the rub;   10
For in that sleep of death what dreams may come
When we have shuffled off this mortal coil,
Must give us pause. There's the respect
That makes calamity of so long life;
For who would bear the whips and scorns of time,
The oppressor's wrong, the proud man's contumely,
The pangs of dispriz'd love, the law's delay,
The insolence of office, and the spurns
That patient merit of the unworthy takes,
When he himself might his quietus make   20
With a bare bodkin? who would fardels bear,
To grunt and sweat under a weary life,
But that the dread of something after death,
The undiscover'd country from whose bourn
No traveller returns, puzzles the will,
And makes us rather bear those ills we have
Than fly to others that we know not of?
Thus conscience does make cowards of us all;
And thus the native hue of resolution
Is sicklied o'er with the pale cast of thought,   30
And enterprises of great pith and moment
With this regard their currents turn awry,
And lose the name of action. Soft you now!
The fair Ophelia! Nymph, in thy orisons
Be all my sins remember'd.

The speech is generally taken to be a pondering on the problems of suicide – but a study of the metre suggests that it is more than this.

ACTIVITY 2

1 Look at the first line. It starts off regularly enough, but how many syllables are there in the line? Then look at the next few lines. Where do you find the first regular line?

2 Now go through the whole speech, counting syllables and listening to stresses.

So far, you've been gathering evidence. Now you have to interpret it.

3 You've probably found some runs of regular lines – those beginning at 'But that the dread', for instance. What do you think the significance is of these? Might they reflect things which have passed through Hamlet's mind before, and he's simply rehearsing the arguments? Look at what he says in these lines, and consider if it's likely.

4 The irregular lines at the beginning of the speech are enough in themselves to suggest a disturbed state of mind – but disturbed about what? The words at the ends of the lines should give you a clue.

5 At line 8, 'consummation' draws attention to itself because of the irregular rhythm of the line. 'Consummation' seems to mean death, in this context, but it's an odd word to use; it is more usually employed in connection with sexual relations in marriage. Which of Hamlet's problems is being suggested here, do you think?

6 Now look at the end of the speech, when Ophelia appears. Why do you think it's irregular here?

Structure

Whichever play you are studying, there are bound to be some structural features to comment on, connected to the playwright's purposes. When you look at the Acts and Scenes in the play as a whole – where they take place, when they take place, in what order they take place, and so on – there are bound to be things to notice.

In *Antony and Cleopatra*, for instance, the action in the early part of the play constantly switches between Egypt and Rome. The audience is bound to compare the two settings, and with them the central characters in each setting, and their language. Structure can be a lot more subtle than this, though. Look at the passage overleaf from the end of Act 5 Scene 1 of *King Richard II*:

KING RICHARD II	Twice for one step I'll groan, the way being short,
	And piece the way out with a heavy heart.
	Come, come, in wooing sorrow let's be brief,
	Since, wedding it, there is such length in grief.
	One kiss shall stop our mouths, and dumbly part;
	Thus give I mine, and thus take I thy heart.
QUEEN	Give me mine own again; 'twere no good part
	To take on me to keep and kill thy heart.
	So, now I have mine own again, be gone,
	That I might strive to kill it with a groan. 10
KING RICHARD II	We make woe wanton with this fond delay:
	Once more, adieu; the rest let sorrow say. [*Exeunt.*]

You might have noticed that this is written in rhyming couplets. In fact, the last 24 lines of the scene are written in this way; this feature of form is part of the structure of the scene. The scene begins with the Queen arriving on the stage with attendants to wait for Richard on his way to prison, and almost certain death. At the end of the scene '*Exeunt*' means 'they go off', but staging decisions have to be made. It's natural for Richard to leave first – he's being taken to prison under guard, after all. This would leave the Queen alone, watching him leave before she departs, in another direction. In this case, the Queen's arrival and exit would bracket the scene – another feature of structure.

This moment is also important in the structure of the whole play. This scene is the first time in the play that the Queen and Richard have spoken together. Up to now she has been more of an observer than someone who acts. At the beginning of this scene, however, she challenges Richard to act, and clearly shows her love for him, which he is shown to return. By the end of Act 4, Richard has been deposed as King by Bolingbroke, and the audience may well feel that the deposition is deserved. If this perception is unaltered by the time he dies, the play may take on the tone of a **morality play**, rather than being a tragedy. In other words Shakespeare needs to create sympathy for Richard.

He does this in Act 5 in a number of ways, with the result that the audience feels affected by his death, which makes the play theatrically richer. Richard is shown to repent his extravagant actions, he fights for his life – and he is shown to be capable of love, and being loved. In this, the Queen is the first and most powerful tool. Shakespeare has them kiss twice in the lines above (you might like to work out exactly where) and as she stands stricken with grief for the man on his way to his death, she has a powerful effect on the audience. Her purpose in the play is, therefore, to act as a structural tool. Through her, Shakespeare *uses structure to shape meanings* about the play.

Language

Shakespeare uses many language techniques to shape meanings: imagery, sound, **syntax** and so on. Here is a reminder of some of the features which you might look for to see how they create meanings.

Language can help to define character. For example, here are the first eleven lines spoken on stage by Caliban, the offspring of a witch, who is kept in servitude by Prospero in *The Tempest*:

> CALIBAN
> As wicked dew as e'er my mother brush'd
> With raven's feather from unwholesome fen
> Drop on you both! a south-west blow on ye,
> And blister you all o'er.
>
> [...]
>
> I must eat my dinner.
> This island's mine, by Sycorax my mother,
> Which thou tak'st from me. When thou camest first,
> Thou strok'dst me and mad'st much of me; wouldst give me
> Water with berries in't; and teach me how
> To name the bigger light, and how the less,   10
> That burn by day and night ...

There are a number of features to notice here, which help to establish Caliban's character. Caliban's first sentence is an exclamation and a curse, as is the second. The syntax is fairly simple. 'I must eat my dinner' is hardly complex, in thought or language. The **diction** – the choice of individual words by the writer – has two noticeable features. It is simple, as in the example above, and in words such as 'takest' and 'camest'. It reflects a simple mind, which struggles to find the words for sun and moon. The language is aggressive, too. 'Wicked', 'blister', and 'unwholesome' show this, while 'raven' and 'fen' are words which have associations with evil and corruption.

You might expect to look for imagery when you think about language, and there isn't much here; but that has implications in itself, suggesting that Caliban thinks too simply and literally to use figurative language. The opening comparison is probably literal, as is 'the bigger light and ... the less'. 'I must eat my dinner' is actually a metaphor – Caliban is stating that he has to do what he is told, for fear of punishment. This is revealing in itself: Caliban's metaphor is drawn from a simple, basic activity.

From the same play, overleaf are the opening words spoken by Miranda, Prospero's daughter:

MIRANDA   If by your art, my dearest father, you have
           Put the wild waters in this roar, allay them.
           The sky, it seems, would pour down stinking pitch,
           But that the sea, mounting to th' welkin's cheek,
           Dashes the fire out. O, I have suffer'd
           With those that I saw suffer: a brave vessel,
           Who had, no doubt, some noble creatures in her,
           Dash'd all to pieces. O, the cry did knock
           Against my very heart. Poor souls, they perish'd.
           Had I been any god of power, I would   10
           Have sunk the sea within the earth, or e'er
           It should the good ship so have swallow'd and
           The fraughting souls within her.

ACTIVITY 3

The language features in Miranda's speech form a sharp contrast with those chosen for Caliban.

- Look at the first sentence. This isn't a curse; what is it?

- The syntax, though not particularly complex, is different from Caliban's. Can you identify phrases which qualify feelings and ideas? What does this tell you about Miranda?

- The diction is a little less simple: 'welkin' and 'fraughting' are not words which Caliban might have used. The dominant tone, created by the diction, is very different. Beginning from 'my dearest father' in the first line, find the words which are strikingly different, in either meaning or association, from Caliban's aggression. Again, what does this reveal about Miranda?

- Identify any imagery used by Miranda. What does 'the cry did knock against my very heart' reveal about Miranda?

Language, then, is one of the means used by the playwright to reveal character. But sometimes the language might change, and in doing so reveal something more about the writer's concerns. In the case of Caliban, for instance, his speech in Act 3 Scene 2 beginning:

Be not afeard: the isle is full of noises,
Sounds and sweet airs, that give delight, and hurt not

shows a different side to him. His final words in the play, 'I'll be wise hereafter, and seek for grace' come rather out of the blue, but his words in his penultimate scene are revealing. 'Good my lord, give me thy favour still. Be patient', 'speak softly', and so on, sound more like Prospero's diction than Caliban's. If Shakespeare is suggesting a change in Caliban by this language, it is a significant one: patience and grace are key ideas in his last plays. Here he is using language (and structure) to express meanings central to his drama.

Language can also be used to make the audience aware of the playwright's concerns. The imagery of blood and darkness which runs through the text of *Macbeth*, for instance, is central to the play's meaning, as is the imagery of blindness in *King Lear*.

Here is a passage from Act 2 Scene 4 of *Macbeth*:

> ROSS   Ah! good father,
> Thou seest, the heavens, as troubled with man's act,
> Threaten his bloody stage: by the clock 'tis day,
> And yet dark night strangles the travelling lamp.
> Is't night's predominance, or the day's shame,
> That darkness does the face of earth entomb,
> When living light should kiss it?

This speech, from a relatively minor character, and not in a crucial moment of the action, nevertheless uses the dominant bloody imagery of the play. This is typical of Shakespeare. The heavens 'threaten' the earth, where man's actions take place, and which Shakespeare typically refers to as a 'stage'. This stage is 'bloody', though. The blood is literal, in the sense that murders have already taken place on the stage (of the theatre), but the evocation of a blood-red stage is powerful. The heavens, disturbed by unnatural acts, produce unnatural darkness in daytime. Shakespeare chooses to mention darkness twice by referring to 'dark night', which 'strangles' the sun. The darkness is murderous, and the metaphor 'lamp' for the sun makes it seem weak by comparison. Night is dominant, the day ashamed, and the enveloping darkness is once again associated with death, through the use of the word 'entomb'. The 'face' of the earth is a very conventional personification, but here the idea of it being entombed suggests a suffocating death. The personification is sharpened by the use of the word 'kiss' in the next line.

Now look at this passage from Act 3 Scene 2:

> MACBETH   Come, seeling night,
> Scarf up the tender eye of pitiful day,
> And with thy bloody and invisible hand
> Cancel and tear to pieces that great bond
> Which keeps me pale! Light thickens, and the crow
> Makes wing to the rooky wood;
> Good things of day begin to droop and drowse;
> While night's black agents to their preys do rouse.

ACTIVITY 4

Answer these questions to show how Shakespeare's choices of language create mood.

1 How many references to darkness are there in the first three lines? You'll have to find out the meaning of 'seeling', and to think about 'scarf up'.

2 What characteristics of day are suggested in the second line?

3 Darkness and blood are persistent images throughout the play. How are the two combined in the third line?

4 What does 'Light thickens' suggest to you? Why is the crow making wing to the rooky wood? Think about colour here.

5 How is a move towards evil suggested in the last two lines? Identify the two references to darkness in the last line.

6 The form underlines the effect of the language here. Rhyme connects things for effect. What things are connected by rhyme here? What is the effect of the repeated sound, do you think? How is the sound of 'drowse' prepared for in the line that it ends?

So far, in this module, form, structure and language have been discussed separately. Often, however, the writer uses these tools together to shape meanings, as in the last two lines of the extract above, and in the extract from *Richard II* on page 52. The rhyming couplets at the end of that scene emphasise the togetherness of Richard and his Queen, and therefore the tragedy of their forced parting, and the language ('dumbly part', 'the rest let sorrow say') further reinforces the hopelessness of the situation. There's another example on page 50 in the speech from *Hamlet*.

Although the tasks you have to do in this module, whether in coursework or examination, will not always demand that you deal with all three, it's a good idea to take the opportunity to do so if you can, to show your knowledge of the range of Shakespeare's skills, and your interpretation of how they work.

AO4: articulate independent opinions and judgements

As stated in the Introduction to this book, it is important to remember that the examiner, if you're doing the exam option, or the marker of your coursework essay, is interested in *your* independent opinion. There isn't a 'correct' interpretation of meaning which they have, and you haven't – it's what *you* think that counts.

Of course, just having an opinion isn't enough. You need to argue your point of view and to support your arguments from the text, showing your '*knowledge and understanding*' (AO2i). It's important, therefore, to plan your answers carefully, sequencing ideas logically and looking to develop them as you write. The examples of coursework tasks given in the following pages should help you to see how you might do this, and you will also see how evidence has to be used.

There are two assessment options for this module: coursework and examination. The basic principle of meeting the Assessment Objectives, which has been shown in the preceding pages, is the same for both options, but there are differences in the sorts of tasks which you might choose.

Coursework option

The specification states that you must study *one* Shakespeare play. For coursework, you can choose any Shakespeare play to study in this module, *except*:

- A play which you might choose in Section A of Module 4 of the Advanced Level course, if you go on to complete it. There are six plays in that section, of which three are by Shakespeare; if you had studied one of these plays as part of AS coursework, you could not then study it as an A Level text.

- A play which you studied at Key Stage 3.

- A play which you studied for GCSE.

In other words, you should not choose any text which you have written about before in an exam, or are likely to at the next level.

You have to write a coursework folder consisting of a single piece of work of about 2,000 words. You will write the piece in school or at home, and then it will be marked by your teacher. Finally, the moderator from the Examination Board will look at your work and all the rest from your centre, and decide on a final mark.

It's very important to select a suitable task for your coursework, one which will enable you to meet the Assessment Objectives for the module. You'll need to keep them very firmly in mind as you plan and write your work. You'll need to work with your teacher in choosing the task, and to seek guidance before you hand in your final draft. Before looking at the sort of task you might choose in this module, and how you might tackle it, here's some advice about the production of coursework which might be useful to you whatever you decide to do.

Producing coursework

There are several things to think about here. Whatever you do, you'll need to think about Assessment Objectives 1 and 2i as you write; but you also need to find a task which deals with the ways in which Shakespeare's '*choices of form, structure and language shape meanings*', (AO3), and which enables you to '*articulate independent opinions and judgements*' (AO4) if you are going to do well. Your task needs to be achievable, too – if you're setting out to write a 2,000-word piece, there's no point in setting yourself a task which can't be done in less than 10,000. As a general rule, the more sharply defined the task is, the better.

You'll probably read the text in class, where you'll have the chance to discuss it with your teacher and other students. But just like preparing your exam texts, you'll need to read it again yourself too. You need to show *'knowledge and understanding'* of the text (AO2i) in your writing, and the more you read it the better you will know it, and the more you'll understand it. This will enable you to analyse the text most effectively, and to support your views.

You need to *plan* your piece of coursework carefully. There are three points to bear in mind here:

1 Spend time on your plan to produce a logical sequence of ideas, which develop an argument and lead to a clear conclusion.

2 Check your plan against the Assessment Objectives – is it clear how and when you are going to achieve them?

3 Because you don't want to have to change your plan much once you start writing, it's worth thinking about length again at this stage. By the time your plan is fleshed out with argument and evidence, does it look as though the word length will be about right? If not, it's worth changing your plan at this stage.

Research may well involve reading articles or essays about your text, from books or the internet, but the most important source of information is still the primary source – the text itself. When you have read secondary sources as part of your research, you must mention them in a bibliography at the end of your essay.

This module carries 30% of the marks for the AS course. Eight of these 30 percentage points are for the ability to *'communicate clearly the knowledge, understanding and insight appropriate to literary study, using appropriate terminology and accurate and coherent written expression'* (AO1). As long as you give yourself plenty of time to write, you can take more care over the accuracy and clarity of your writing than you can in an exam: you can check it, revise it and improve it when you've finished the first draft. There are specific marks allocated for this, as you can see, so take advantage of them.

Ten of the 30 percentage points are available for Assessment Objective 2i – the ability to *'respond with knowledge and understanding to a literary text'*. Your *understanding* will be shown by the quality of your argument; but *knowledge* has to underpin everything you write, in exams or coursework. In coursework you have the leisure to practise what you have to do under time pressure in the exams, that is, to provide support for what you say from the text. You can demonstrate knowledge by referring to details or echoes of the text, or by quotation. Short quotations (which are usually the most effective) can be included in the body of your writing, while longer quotations can be written on separate lines, so that they're more easily read. If you're quoting lines of verse, you need to indicate the line divisions. Here's an example from *The Winter's Tale* showing how these conventions work:

Before the final moment, Paulina protests twice about the perception that any magic she might perform might be sinful: she refers to 'wicked powers' and 'unlawful business', recalling Prospero's firm 'no' when similarly accused in <u>The Tempest</u>. After the statue moves, Leontes is clear in her defence:

If this be magic, let it be an art
Lawful as eating.

If you're quoting from a secondary source, such as a critic, this should be footnoted, by numbering the quotation and providing the source of the quotation, either at the foot of the page or at the end of the essay.

'How literally should the audience take this moment? Bloom's view is that Paulina, while "making reasonably clear that she is not a necromancer, is also careful to distance us from realism".[1]

1. *The Invention of the Human* by Harold Bloom, Fourth Estate, 1999, p. 660.

If you use the words of other writers such as critics in your own writing, you *must* acknowledge them. You have to sign a declaration that the coursework is your own work, and if you 'lift' from other writing without acknowledging it, it is called malpractice, and you may lose all your marks for the module.

When you have completed a first draft of your coursework essay, your teacher may allow you to redraft it, as long as there is enough time to do so. Your teacher is only allowed to give general advice and guidelines as to how you might improve the work, not to correct or rewrite it. Of course, you should heed any advice that you are offered, but basically you should aim for your first draft to be as good as you can make it. It's a lot easier to make minor changes than major ones.

AS coursework submissions should be approximately 2,000 words long. You should be careful not to exceed this limit casually. If your first draft comes to 2,400 words, you can probably cut it fairly easily, and you may want your teacher's guidance about which parts to prune. If it is 4,000 words, though, you're in trouble – cutting sentences here and there, and tightening expression, won't cut it by 50 per cent. This means you have either made a mistake in selecting the task, or at the planning stage, or when you were partway through. Your teacher will give you coursework deadlines, and it's important to stick to them – not just to please your teacher, but to improve your chances of success. You will only be able to cut/redraft/rethink if you've got the time to do it.

Coursework tasks

The list of coursework tasks which follows, and the ways of tackling them, are by no means exhaustive. The tasks simply illustrate some ways of planning and writing successful coursework essays, while keeping the Assessment Objectives firmly in focus. Reading through them may well make you think of tasks you can tackle for your chosen text, or of completely different tasks which access the objectives.

Looking at part of the text

One valuable way of approaching coursework is to analyse a particular passage from the play you're studying, and relate it to the whole play – a technique you'll need to master if you are entering for the exam option. Think about where the passage belongs in the dramatic and thematic structure of the play. How do you think the words and actions reverberate in the rest of the play? What is there in the language of the extract which has significance for the whole play, in your opinion?

As an example of how you might go about a task like this, here's the first scene of *The Tempest*, followed by an activity which could lead to a coursework assignment:

The Tempest Act 1 Scene 1

On a ship at sea. A tempestuous noise of thunder and lightning heard.

[*Enter a* MASTER *and a* BOATSWAIN *severally.*]

MASTER	Boatswain!
BOATSWAIN	Here, master: what cheer?
MASTER	Good, speak to the mariners: fall to't, yarely, or we run ourselves aground: bestir, bestir.

[*Exit.*]

[*Enter* MARINERS.]

BOATSWAIN	Heigh, my hearts! cheerly, cheerly, my hearts! yare, yare! Take in the topsail. Tend to the master's whistle. Blow, till thou burst thy wind, if room enough!	10

[*Enter* ALONSO, SEBASTIAN, ANTONIO, FERDINAND, GONZALO, *and others.*]

ALONSO	Good boatswain, have care. Where's the master? Play the men.	
BOATSWAIN	I pray now, keep below.	
ANTONIO	Where is the master, boatswain?	
BOATSWAIN	Do you not hear him? You mar our labour: keep your cabins: you do assist the storm.	20
GONZALO	Nay, good, be patient.	
BOATSWAIN	When the sea is. Hence! What cares these roarers for the name of king? To cabin: silence! trouble us not.	
GONZALO	Good, yet remember whom thou hast aboard.	
BOATSWAIN	None that I more love than myself. You are a counsellor: if you can command these elements to silence, and work the peace of the present, we will not hand a rope more; use your authority: if you cannot, give thanks you have lived so long, and make yourself ready in your cabin for the mischance of the hour, if it so hap. Cheerly, good hearts! Out of our way, I say.	30

[*Exit.*]

GONZALO   I have great comfort from this fellow: methinks he
           hath no drowning mark upon him; his complexion is
           perfect gallows. Stand fast, good Fate, to his
           hanging! make the rope of his destiny our cable,
           for our own doth little advantage. If he be not
           born to be hanged, our case is miserable.

           [*Exeunt.*]   40

           [*Re-enter* BOATSWAIN.]

BOATSWAIN Down with the topmast! yare! lower, lower! Bring
           her to try with main-course. [*A cry within.*] A plague upon
           this howling! they are louder than the weather, or our office.

           [*Re-enter* SEBASTIAN, ANTONIO, *and* GONZALO.]

           Yet again! what do you here? Shall we give o'er
           and drown? Have you a mind to sink?

SEBASTIAN A pox o' your throat, you bawling, blasphemous,
           incharitable dog!   50

BOATSWAIN Work you then.

ANTONIO   Hang, cur! hang, you whoreson, insolent noisemaker,
           we are less afraid to be drowned than thou art.

GONZALO   I'll warrant him for drowning; though the ship were
           no stronger than a nutshell, and as leaky as an
           unstanched wench.

BOATSWAIN Lay her a-hold, a-hold! Set her two courses; off to
           sea again; lay her off.

           [*Enter* MARINERS, *wet.*]

MARINERS   All lost! to prayers, to prayers! all lost! [*Exeunt.*]   60

BOATSWAIN What, must our mouths be cold?

GONZALO   The king and prince at prayers! let's assist them,
           For our case is as theirs.

SEBASTIAN I am out of patience.

ANTONIO   We are merely cheated of our lives by drunkards:
           This wide-chapp'd rascal – would thou mightst lie drowning,
           The washing of ten tides!

GONZALO   He'll be hang'd yet,
           Though every drop of water swear against it
           And gape at wid'st to glut him.   70

           [*A confused noise within*: 'Mercy on us!' –
           'We split, we split!' – 'Farewell, my wife and
           children!' –
           'Farewell, brother!' – 'We split, we split, we split!']

ANTONIO	Let's all sink wi' the king.
SEBASTIAN	Let's take leave of him.
	[*Exeunt* ANTONIO *and* SEBASTIAN.]
GONZALO	Now would I give a thousand furlongs of sea for an acre of barren ground; long heath, brown furze, any thing. The wills above be done! but I would fain die a dry death.

80

[*Exeunt.*]

An interesting way to start thinking about the scene would be to consider which words you would want the audience to hear if you were directing the play. This is a very practical question: in a naturalistic staging of the first scene, it's likely that much of the dialogue would be drowned out by the noise of the thunder and the sea.

ACTIVITY 5

Working alone or in a group, identify which words are most important for the audience to hear and why. As you work, consider the following points:

- **Plot**. What do the audience need to know here that is important to an understanding of events later in the play?

- **Character**. It's unlikely that the audience will make much of individual characters in this scene, but its impact suggests that something will be remembered. Which lines or actions say something significant about the characters? It may not just be about individual characters – you might want to consider how the nobles and the seamen behave towards each other. Do all the noblemen behave in the same way? How do their words and actions foreshadow what we learn of them later?

- **Meanings**. Some words or ideas in the scene are found elsewhere in the play. For instance, Gonzalo's exclamation 'The wills above be done' is not only typical of his attitude and character, but introduces the idea of a controlling power beyond Prospero that is examined many times in the play, for example in Act II: 'Heavens rain grace on that which breeds between 'em'.

- **Language**. The scene is in prose, which is perhaps unsurprising given the frantic, disordered atmosphere which Shakespeare is creating here. There are words, though, which may have echoes elsewhere in the play. For example, Sebastian remarks 'I'm out of patience' – typical of him, we come to learn, but the word 'patience' takes on a wider significance, particularly in the final scene, as shown in the lines overleaf:

ALONSO	Irreparable is the loss, and patience Says it is past her cure.
PROSPERO	I rather think You have not sought her help; of whose soft grace, For the like loss I have her sovereign aid, And rest myself content.

The connection between loss, patience and grace made here is not only significant in this play, but in all of Shakespeare's last plays. In Act 5 of *The Winter's Tale*, for instance, exactly the same sequence and type of language is invoked. Look for other examples of language which occur again later in the play.

Working through an exercise like this should provide you with the material to write an essay about Act 1 Scene 1 in relation to the rest of the play, drawing evidence from the passage and elsewhere in the play, as above. You need to show *knowledge* and *understanding* of the play as well as writing about form, structure *and* language. Although the idea for this essay is based on the first scene of the play, it is obvious that you couldn't write an adequate answer without knowledge and understanding of the entire play.

A variation on this approach could be to find a single key line, and show how it reverberates through the play in a number of ways.

ACTIVITY 6

Look at the context of the line 'Are you our daughter?' from *King Lear*, Act 1 Scene 4 and then try to answer the following questions.

FOOL	So out went the candle, and we were left darkling.
LEAR	Are you our daughter?
GONERIL	I would you would make use of your good wisdom …

1 Think about the significance of this moment in the plot. What does Lear start to realise, that the audience already knows? Where does this lead?

2 Think about the significance of the question itself. Who is Lear's true daughter? In what sense?

3 The corollary to 'Who are you?' is 'Who am I?' What does this moment start to reveal to Lear about himself?

4 What is happening to Lear's power here? What significance does this have in the context of the whole play? Notice that Goneril's reply is not an answer to the question at all.

5 Lear is questioning what he sees in front of him, with his own eyes, as it were. Perhaps this is the beginning of him being able to 'see straight'. This scene obviously has a huge bearing on one of the central themes of the play, and its associated language, both for Lear's story and the blinding of Gloucester. How is the line 'I stumbled when I saw' (Act 4 Scene 1) relevant to this?

6 The choice of words is interesting, too, especially when compared with Lear's words in Act 4, when he wakes up from madness and recognises Cordelia: 'I think this lady/To be my child Cordelia'. Notice that every word from 'Are you our daughter' has changed: 'our' has become 'my', 'daughter' has become 'child', and so on. Why? What does it tell you about Lear's state of mind, and his change in attitude?

7 'Are you our daughter?' is a half line of verse – the line is incomplete; Goneril's response forms a new line of verse. What happens in the pause created, do you think? Who are the audience looking at? What might Lear be thinking?

If you don't know *King Lear* well you won't have been able to answer all the questions fully, but the Activity will have given you some idea of the scope of features to look for.

ACTIVITY 7

In your chosen play, look for a line which resonates in the text like the one from *King Lear* above, so that you can open up a number of aspects of the play. You should look for a line which is significant in some of these ways:

• form/structure/language

• plot

• character and relationships

• meanings

• action.

Remember that your aim is to write about the line in relation to the rest of the play, showing your *knowledge and understanding*, and that a significant part of this must relate to *form*, *structure and language*.

Interpreting an aspect of the text

A straightforward way of developing a coursework task would be to look at a particular aspect of the text you're studying and give your reading of it. Once you've started to think about an interpretation, the essential first step is gathering evidence from the text, through a selective re-reading of the text, noting the passages and lines you might use.

Clearly, there are many aspects of your chosen play that you could write about. These could focus on a particular concept in the play and how it is presented. The concept might be peculiar to this play, or it might be one that is found in several of Shakespeare's plays. Some examples are:

- kingship
- justice
- appearance and reality
- time

- fate
- redemption
- the nature of tragedy
- the nature of love.

You could equally choose to look at dramatic features of the text in other ways. Examples might be how the worlds of Rome and Egypt are presented in *Antony and Cleopatra*, how magic is used in *The Tempest*, how women are presented in *Richard III*, or how *The Taming of the Shrew* might be made relevant to a modern audience.

ACTIVITY 8

Choose an aspect of your chosen play to write about, which you think could form the basis of a coursework assignment of 2,000 words. Follow these stages to complete the task.

1 Read the text again selectively, looking for passages relevant to your idea.

2 Make a note of useful evidence (lines from the text) as you work.

3 Review your task in the light of what you've read and found. Will it still work? Is it too slight a task, or too large?

4 Plan your essay, remembering the three things you have to give evidence of to succeed.

5 Write a first draft. Refer to the advice given in the section 'Producing coursework' to help you.

Although the choice might seem very wide when looked at like this, it's vital to remember what you have to show to produce a successful answer. You must deal a) with the ways in which writers' choices of form, structure and language shape meanings, b) you must offer your independent opinion or judgement, and c) you must respond with knowledge and understanding. Part of *knowledge and understanding* which you could lose sight of in this kind of task is the very form of the text you're dealing with. The text is a *play*, and you need to think about how the aspect of the play you have chosen to write about is presented *dramatically*.

Offering an interpretation

Whichever task you decide to do for coursework, it's important that you show your 'independent opinion' (AO4), as this is tested here. You may choose to put this first in your selection of task. Of course, it's not enough to have an interesting idea about the text. You must argue your interpretation with evidence that can show your knowledge and understanding. Once you've started to think about an interpretation, the essential first step is to gather evidence from the text.

Gathering evidence from the text

Let's suppose that you decide to write about the women in *Hamlet* and choose to show that they are surprisingly frail in character. The title could be:

'Frailty, thy name is woman'. How far do you think Hamlet's remark is true of the ways women are presented in the play?

Here's some of the evidence you might use – it's up to you to decide how to use it to make your case.

Gertrude

- Hamlet says that she 'would hang on him/As if increase of appetite had grown/By what it fed on.' He says that she 'posts with such dexterity to incestuous sheets'.

- The Ghost says that Claudius 'won to his shameful lust/The will of my most seeming virtuous Queen'; and 'so lust, though to a radiant angel link'd/Will sat itself in a celestial bed/And prey on garbage.' He describes the throne of Denmark as 'a couch for luxury and damned incest'.

A clear picture of this woman appears in these lines. Of course, the views of the two characters who say the lines may be biased, but she does remarry very quickly.

- Look at her own words. When she considers the Player Queen, she doesn't regard her as honest, but rather cynically: 'The lady doth protest too much, methinks'. When she thinks about Ophelia's death, her thoughts move quickly to the marriage bed: 'I hop'd thou should'st have been my Hamlet's wife:/I thought thy bride-bed to have deck'd …'

- What about her behaviour towards her son? Her first words to him in the play tell him to forget his father: 'do not for ever … seek for thy noble father in the dust'.

She goes along with the use of Rosencrantz and Guildenstern, the Claudius/Polonius plot to watch him with Ophelia to see how he behaves, and the introduction of a spy into her bedchamber. She allows Polonius to tell her how to behave. Claudius is sure that she will not be an obstacle in the plan to murder Hamlet (Act 4 Scene 7).

Ophelia

- Look at her words: 'I do not know, my lord, what I should think'. She is instructed by her father not to talk to Hamlet: 'I shall obey, my lord'; 'I did repel his letters, and denied his access to me'. 'This in obedience hath my daughter shown me', says Polonius.

- Look at her behaviour. Like Gertrude, she goes along with the plot to discover the source of Hamlet's madness, allowing herself to be used in it. She returns her 'remembrances' to Hamlet, so that Claudius and Polonius can see the effect. How much does she love him?

- She says of herself that she is 'of ladies most deject and wretched', and 'Oh woe is me!' Who is she sorry for?

Having selected this evidence, you could make a case that shows both of these women as weak and morally suspect. To demonstrate your understanding, though, you need to look for the apparent flaws in your case and then try to fit them to your interpretation. The obvious problem is the audience's impression of the two women, especially in the light of Ophelia's madness and death and Gertrude's report of it. What can you say that will anticipate these objections?

- Look at the scene where Hamlet jumps into Ophelia's grave. Once he's done so, how much does he say about his feelings for Ophelia?

- Look carefully at the report of Ophelia's death in Act 4 Scene 7. Was her death a deliberate act?

- Shakespeare presents Gertrude very favourably here, quite deliberately. He gives the report of the death to her, though anybody could have delivered it. The speech is full of pathos and beautiful imagery, a deliberate choice that affects the way the audience thinks about Ophelia and Gertrude. The dialogue and verse are manipulated so that the account ends with Gertrude saying 'drown'd, drown'd', the only two words on the line. What is the audience looking at and thinking in the pause created before the next line?

Does all this undermine your earlier argument? What was Shakespeare doing with this scene? Perhaps if we feel more sympathetic towards her, this helps to accentuate the tragedy of Hamlet's loss when she dies and the treachery of Claudius. But you could argue that this doesn't change her earlier behaviour.

Writing the assignment

You must plan this piece carefully. You may well have had an opinion about the issue before you started selecting and reviewing evidence, and this process has helped to finalise, or even change it. You will need to plan the structure of the assignment with your opinion firmly in mind – it should be evident at the beginning, and should inform everything that you write. 'How far' in the wording of the task, though, suggests that evidence has to be weighed carefully to reach 'judgements', another word drawn from AO4. The evidence, of course, will have to lean heavily on *the ways in which writers' choices of form, structure and language shape meanings* (AO3). Most of the evidence referred to above is exactly this.

Critical analysis of a particular production seen

This might well be a popular choice. After all, the best way to understand the plays as theatre is to see and hear them in the environment for which they were written. You should always seize the chance to see a production of a play you're studying if you can, so why not make it the basis of a coursework assignment?

If this looks like an easy option, think again. You need to do much more than simply describe the production. You must remember that the key Assessment Objectives which you have to address in this module are:

- to show detailed understanding of the ways in which writers' choices of form, structure and language shape meanings

- to articulate informed independent opinions and judgements.

You have to show evidence of these in your writing, so they need to be in your mind when you see the production. You should have a firm idea of what you're looking for (see below), and it is useful to jot some things down immediately after the play – better than writing notes during the play, when there's so much to see and hear. It's even better, of course, if you can see a production twice, to build on what you saw the first time.

To see how this might work, look at this example. A 1995 production of *Macbeth* had these key features of presentation:

- Lady Macbeth was shown as pregnant. This was clear from her first appearance, and became more pronounced, so that the signs of a miscarriage were evident in the sleepwalking scene.

- The witches were on stage for most of the action, because they played all the parts without names (and Seyton), as well as their own.

Lady Macbeth's pregnancy made her seem even more callous at times. 'I would . . . Have pluck'd my nipple from his boneless gums/And dash'd the brains out' seemed more real and more chilling from a pregnant woman. The blood on her legs in the sleepwalking scene, though horrible, made sense of her suicide and madness. The relationship between the Macbeths achieved an unusual sort of intimacy, and affected the physicality between them. When Macbeth was broken by his wife in Act 1 Scene 7, he fell to his knees and was pulled in to the visibly pregnant stomach on 'We fail?', suggesting a different sort of sexual relationship and control to the one usually chosen.

The witches' presence on stage kept them at the centre of the action, observing and prompting. They became more controlling and omniscient, a part of the action, not separate from it. For instance, the play began with all the male characters on stage, ready for Act 1 Scene 2. The witches (two played by men, one by a woman) were dressed as part of the army, and were picked out by spotlights for the opening lines. They brought down the lights for the interval, too, and for the end of the play: as soldiers again, they were left on stage with Macbeth's head and sword when Malcolm's army departed. The *structure* of the play was altered by the idea for the ending. The play now opened and was ended by the witches, which again emphasised their control.

Lady Macbeth's pregnancy had a bearing on the theme of children in the play. It gave force to Macbeth's concern about the 'barren sceptre' placed in his hand, 'no son of mine succeeding', and his horror at the vision of Banquo's crowned descendants. The vision of the 'bloody child' might have meant Macduff's child – but the tragic culmination of Lady Macbeth's pregnancy produced another meaning.

The greatest effect on the *meaning* of the play came as a result of the presentation of the witches. Because they watched over Macbeth all the time, and prompted him to some extent – throwing the dagger into the stage for him to find, for instance – they seemed to be more in control, and therefore took some of the responsibility for his evil deeds from him. This was particularly clear in Act 5. The decision to play witches as all the unnamed characters meant that Macbeth was surrounded by witches in his castle – everybody else had left, of course. This created more sympathy for Macbeth, perhaps, but also altered the nature of the play.

Writing the assignment

Seeing and hearing these features of the play would have helped you to write a critical analysis of the production, focusing on the appropriate skills. One way to approach *independent opinions and judgements* here would have been to measure the features of the production against your expectations, based on your knowledge of the play. You might have written about what was gained and lost by this interpretation, and whether the play worked dramatically. You might have written about staging elements such as costume and set – but remember, you would have to relate these elements to the interpretation being offered, and your view of the play. You have to address *form, structure and language*, too. You might have done this by providing your view of elements of the play, or by showing how the structure was affected by the interpretation, or how particular words and phrases became important in the production.

Attending a performance

When you attend a performance of a play with a view to writing about it as a piece of coursework, you need to go about it in an organised way if you're going to get the best out of it.

1   Before you go

- You're presumably already familiar with the play, but if you haven't looked at it for a while, remind yourself of it, and think about what you might be expecting to see and hear on the stage.

- Remember that the key Assessment Objectives here are 2i, 3 and 4. What you eventually write will have to relate to these Objectives.

2   At the performance

It's best not to jot things down during the performance – your eyes and ears should be on the stage. If you are going to write anything down, it should be very brief – you can make sense of it afterwards. You could use the interval, if there is one. Here's a list of the sort of things you should be looking for as you watch:

Stage interpretations. Look for any ideas which have informed the production, which suggest how the director and cast want the audience to see the play. Clues to these might be found in:

- the presentation of characters and relationships

- features of language – the way words and lines are spoken, and any particular words or phrases which are made to 'stand out' in some way

- the way the plot and action are managed – are there any cuts? changes in sequencing?

- is the set representational? What does it represent or suggest? Does it suggest a particular time period – and does that have a bearing on what the audience think about the action?

- do the costume and props assist the interpretation?

Settings. Looking at the set, costume and props together will reveal something about the setting, and what the production is saying about the play. If the play is set in a different time period from the original performances, this may make the audience think differently about the ideas in the play. This could be reflected not just in the 'dressing' – costume, set, props – but in the way the actors relate to each other in movement and speech.

Your response. In all of this, you need to have your critical faculties alert. How are you responding to what you see? Why?

3   After the performance

Unless you're going to start writing your assignment straight away, now is the time to make some notes, while the performance is still fresh in your mind. Think about the list of points above and anything else that struck you about the production. It's helpful to speak to other people as well at this stage, as they may have seen things that you didn't which might be helpful, or they might have interpreted the production differently. If there are reviews of the production available, read them too, as they may express different interpretations, or different attitudes to the performance.

4 Practising skills

You may not have the luxury of seeing another play before you see the one you're going to write about, but if you do, you could go through this process as a trial run. Or you could apply part of the approach to TV drama or a film version of the play you're studying.

Comparing film and theatre versions

If you have the opportunity to see two productions of a play, this could form an excellent basis for an essay. It's more likely, though, that you might compare a film version to a stage production. With a canvas as large as this, you could choose to narrow the focus of your essay to a particular aspect of the versions. Balancing the two interpretations in the productions, with evidence, and arguing your own view of the play in relation to these two, with evidence showing knowledge and understanding, will meet the requirements of Assessment Objectives 2i and 4. You still need to include *understanding of the ways in which writers' choices of form, structure and language shape meanings*, though, either with evidence from the text or in the way the versions highlight some of these features. Here's how you might go about it.

The process of analysing the stage production would be exactly the same as that suggested above. For the second version you see, though, whether it's stage or screen, part of your observation will be of differences from the first version.

Looking at film is rather different from looking at a stage – particularly if you choose a film version which isn't just a recording of a stage version – and will give you a sharper difference to write about. Here are some ideas for the sort of choices you might make.

- If you were studying *The Tempest*, and had the chance to see a stage production of the play, there are several film versions available on video which you could study alongside the production. The BBC version, with Michael Hordern, offers a fairly conventional reading of the play, with settings quite close to a stage set. At the same time, however, the androgynous representation of Ariel, and the attitudes of Prospero, offer material for discussion of different interpretations. The filming of the opening and the appearances of Ariel and the other spirits would probably be very different from the stage version. Two more unconventional films of the play are directed by Derek Jarman, and Peter Greenaway, whose adaptation has the title *Prospero's Books*. Both treat the play in quite startling ways, and offer much to discuss and write about. An interesting choice might be to look at one of these two films, the BBC version, and a stage production.

- There are several film versions of *Macbeth* available, too. Roman Polanski's film and the recording of the RSC studio production with Ian McKellen and

Judi Dench are quite different, and offer strong interpretations of the relationships between characters. Comparing either or both of these with a stage production would be a viable option.

- The Japanese director Kurosawa's *Ran* is his film version of *King Lear* and would form an excellent basis for a comparison with a stage production – not only in some unusual interpretations, but also for the Japanese setting which the director uses so cleverly to affect the audience's view of the play.

Watching a film to compare with a play

Much of your attention will be on the same elements as in a stage production (see 'Attending a performance', page 70). Interpretations, and the ways that characters' relationships, setting, costume, etc., develop them, will still be high on your agenda.

There are other elements to look at, though, which are peculiar to film. You need to consider:

1 Use of *setting/place*. Film offers more opportunity than stage, generally speaking, for using a variety of places. Has this been done, and what effect do the settings have on the view of the play being presented?

2 *Lighting/colour*. Because of the nature of the medium, concentration on particular colours, or lighting effects peculiar to cinema, can be used. What do you notice, and why are these colours/effects being used?

3 *Camera distance and angle*. Apart from promenade productions, the angle of the audience member to the stage doesn't alter much, but in film long and short shots, close-ups, panning and tracking shots, and a variety of angles can all be used. The camera techniques that you should look for are those that clearly enhance a particular moment or line in the play. You can then use this in a discussion of *language*.

4 *Cutting/fading*. Film offers a number of techniques for moving from scene to scene, or moment to moment, which are not open to a theatre director. A technique like cut or fade might have been used not simply to speed the action, but to create an effect – perhaps by juxtaposing one moment, event or character sharply against another. Again, it's these motives you should be thinking about once you've identified the technique.

5 *Music/sound*. Of course, music and sound may well be used in the stage production that you see, but music and sound effects are often used more extensively in film. If this is so, what effects do they achieve? Try to be as exact as you can.

6 *Special effects*. A play with 'magic' elements, such as *Macbeth*, *The Tempest*, or *A Midsummer Night's Dream* might well be filmed using

---

> special effects – and techniques peculiar to film such as split-screen shots could be used in any play. If these techniques have been used, try to work out what the film director's purpose might have been.
>
> **7** *Soliloquies.* A feature of most of the Shakespeare plays that you are likely to study is the soliloquy – speeches made by a character when alone on the stage, which enable the audience to see and hear the character's thoughts clearly. Both *form* and *language* are involved here. How have these passages been delivered in the film version?

The danger in writing about a film version of the play(s) you're studying is that you might be tempted to write about the film only as a film. There's no point in writing about any of the techniques above without relating them to *purpose*, that is, the motives of the director in making the audience see the play in a particular way. Remember that it's the play which has to be the centre of your discussion.

Writing the assignment

Because you're focusing on comparing the two versions and the interpretations they offer, your plan should reflect this. You need to give your own view, too, both of the productions and the play. Here are four possible ways of approaching the assignment.

1
  - an analysis of version 1
  - an analysis of version 2
  - comparison/contrast of the two versions
  - your view

2
  - an analysis of version 1
  - an analysis of version 2, comparing and contrasting as you go
  - your view

3
  - an analysis of versions 1 and 2 together, comparing and contrasting features as you go
  - your view

4
  - an introduction using your overview, both of text and versions
  - an analysis of versions 1 and 2 together, comparing and contrasting features as you go, and using your views as indicators
  - a conclusion, evaluating the comparative success of the versions.

Any of these approaches could succeed. Remember that in writing the essay you will need to show knowledge as well as understanding, by using details not only from the productions but from the text(s) themselves.

Proposals for staging the text

This is an attractive option, in that it will allow you to think about the play both practically and creatively. There are some dangers, though. There would be no point in writing simply about costume, setting, stage action, or any other feature of staging without relating them to your interpretation of the play – your *informed independent judgement*. You must show *knowledge and understanding*, too, so your suggestions need to be referenced in the text, and you must address some features of *form, structure and language*.

Another danger is writing too much. You should not try to write a full production script, working through the play chronologically: the outcome would inevitably be long and repetitive. It's the principles of staging your interpretation that you're concerned with – the different production elements should be seen in this light. You'll probably want to consider some key scenes or moments from the play, so that you can focus on particular features of form or language.

In the third suggestion for a coursework task, on page ooo above, the example of a production of *Macbeth* featured a particular interpretation of the witches. If you had come up with this idea, you can see that your interpretation would have necessitated the following staging elements:

- How they were dressed – they would have to be in a variety of costumes to suit the parts they played, such as soldiers, waiting gentlewomen, and so on.

- The gender of the players – in this production, there was only one female witch, and two males, one white and one black. This in itself offered a variety of role playing.

- How they behaved – their degree of control was indicated by the way they seemed to command the lighting, and the throwing of the dagger into the stage for Macbeth to find.

- The management of the action – this would be very noticeable to the audience, as they closed both halves of the play.

- The effects on stage of their presentation. It was mentioned that in Act 5 they surrounded Macbeth, and stage positioning would emphasise this. This in its turn, together with the other elements above, would suggest an interpretation of Macbeth – that his responsibility for his evil deeds was lessened by their evident control.

ACTIVITY 9

Using your text, think about how you would like to present the play, looking at the range of staging elements listed below and taking into account the play and what you want to do with it. Remember that many modern interpretations have set the plays in quite different places or genres, such as Baz Luhrman's *Romeo and Juliet*, *Ten Things I Hate About You* as a version of *Taming of the Shrew*, or the stage production of *Twelfth Night* which set the play in a Star Trek world.

1 The colour of costumes might be significant, to suggest character, or what the character represents. Obviously period might be significant, too: different settings, which might suggest an interpretation of the text, could be suggested by costume, probably in conjunction with set and props.

2 Male characters don't necessarily have to be played by men, or women by women. Shakespeare's women were played by boys, of course, and in recent times several leading male parts have been played by women, with particular effects: Fiona Shaw played Richard II, for instance, and Kathryn Hunter played King Lear.

3 How the character is 'played', in terms of how the actors behave, speak the lines, and what they choose to emphasise, might be really significant and useful in enabling you to write about language. But remember that whatever you say needs to be linked to your intentions, to what the interpretation is. You might want to suggest that particular words or phrases are picked out by the actor(s), because of the interpretation you're suggesting.

4 In the same way, it will only be valuable to comment on stage action and stage positioning, if you can link it successfully to interpretation – and it's how the audience sees it that's important.

5 It's a good idea to show these staging elements, or some of them, working at particular moments in a scene or part of a scene where this staging and interpretation will be particularly clear.

Writing the assignment

It's important to frame your staging suggestions in the light of the relevant Assessment Objectives. This begins at the thinking stage, and continues with planning. You need to show *knowledge and understanding*, of course, so your suggestions should include quotes from the text, and show a considered and supported view of what it might mean. Your *independent opinion and judgement* will be shown by your interpretation of the play, and you must seek to include some *detailed understanding of the ways writers' choices of form, structure and language shape meanings* in your explanation of your staging suggestions, and in your views on the play as a whole.

Examination option

If you choose the examination option, you will have a choice of three Shakespeare plays and, as this is an open book module, you will be able to take your text into the examination room with you. Broadly, you might be asked two types of question, probably one of each type on each text to choose from. The first type will ask you to look at a single scene, or part of a scene, and to write about its dramatic function, or its importance or significance in the play. The second type will ask you to look at the presentation of an idea or a character in the play as a whole, but might ask you to concentrate on some particular episodes, or to range more widely through the text if you wish. Some examples of the sort of tasks you might face, and how to think about them, are given below, but the skills required in approaching the text are the same as those you've worked on throughout this section.

Looking at a single scene

You might be asked to look at a single scene in the play, and comment on some of its features. You could be asked how you might direct it, too; 'Proposals for staging the text' on page 74 suggests how you might tackle such a task. The sort of features you could be asked about are likely to include details of form, structure and language, presentation of characters and relationships, dramatic effects or functions, and how some of the writer's meanings might appear here. You can see that these relate to Assessment Objectives 2i and 3. Key words like 'how appropriate', 'how would you', and 'consider' will remind you that you have to deal with Assessment Objective 4, too, and offer your *independent opinion and judgement*.

Here are the first 18 lines from *Antony and Cleopatra*. You could be asked to read Act 1 Scene 1 and consider its dramatic effect, and the presentation of the characters of Antony and Cleopatra.

[*Enter* DEMETRIUS *and* PHILO.]

PHILO   Nay, but this dotage of our general's
O'erflows the measure; those his goodly eyes,
That o'er the files and musters of the war
Have glow'd like plated Mars, now bend, now turn,
The office and devotion of their view
Upon a tawny front; his captain's heart,
Which in the scuffles of great fights hath burst
The buckles on his breast, reneges all temper,
And is become the bellows and the fan
To cool a gipsy's lust. Look! where they come: 10

[*Flourish. Enter* ANTONY, CLEOPATRA, *her Ladies, the Train, with Eunuchs fanning her.*]

Take but good note, and you shall see in him
The triple pillar of the world transform'd
Into a strumpet's fool; behold and see.

CLEOPATRA   If it be love indeed, tell me how much.

MARK ANTONY   There's beggary in the love that can be reckon'd.

CLEOPATRA   I'll set a bourn how far to be belov'd.

MARK ANTONY	Then must thou needs find out new heaven, new earth.
	[*Enter an* ATTENDANT.]
ATTENDANT	News, my good lord, from Rome.
MARK ANTONY	Grates me; the sum.

Form, structure, language

The first point here is *structural*. This is the opening of the play, and (typically) the audience are given a view of the central characters before they enter, creating expectation, and giving a context for the appearance, albeit from a Roman point of view. The scene is structured to begin and end with comments from the minor characters before Antony and Cleopatra appear and after they leave; and the whole play ends with comments about them, again from a Roman.

Although this might suggest a Chorus-like function for these characters, the audience are left in no doubt that they are not impartial. They enter in the middle of a conversation, marked by 'Nay, but', and Philo's *language* shows his allegiance to Antony: he is referred to as 'our' general in the first line, and Cleopatra is a 'gipsy' to him. His words are full of military detail: 'files', 'musters', 'plated Mars', 'great fights', 'buckles'. Change is signalled by 'bend' and 'turn', underlined by the form: the repetition of 'now bend, now turn' enables the stresses to fall on the words showing change, and lifts them out for notice. The change is away from 'goodly', though, and is characterised as 'dotage' which 'O'erflows the measure', the first mentions of age and excess, key ideas in the play. Duty is another concept at the heart of the moral discussion, and is also introduced here: Antony's 'office and devotion' have strayed to **sensuality**. The last words before Cleopatra's entrance are pejorative: 'a gipsy's lust', and 'transform'd into a strumpet's fool' follows close behind.

The language of the two central characters initially upholds Philo's view. Despite the grand entrance, their talk is clearly private, and concerns only themselves, i.e. the extent of their love. Their importance, and the sense of something universal beyond them, is nevertheless being signalled by language already: Philo refers to Antony as 'the triple pillar of the world', and finding out 'new heaven, new earth' suggests, through hyperbole, the extent of their passion. Antony's mind is clearly not on his military duty: 'Grates me; the sum' is not only sharp and truncated, but is also emphasised as such by completing the messenger's line. *Form* and *language* work together here.

Dramatic effects

As this is the opening of the play, the audience might expect a dramatic flourish of some sort, in action or words, instead of which they are privy to a conversation which has already begun. The entrance is held back, perhaps making the audience, like Demetrius, anticipate it even more. When it does come, Philo signals its significance and the importance of observing very strongly: 'Look ... Take but good note ... you shall see ... behold and see.' This forms a strong dramatic context for Antony and Cleopatra's opening words. The words are not regal, though, again denying some expectations, perhaps, but are private, bearing out Philo's view of Antony's obsession. His sharpness to the Messenger is dramatic, too: This rudeness does not become Antony as a leader (though we see it several times in the play as characteristic of Cleopatra), and it indicates his dereliction of duty.

You can see that in dealing with just these 18 lines it's possible to examine form, structure and language, presentation of characters and relationships, dramatic effects and functions, and how some of the writer's meanings emerge. In the exam you would probably be asked to look at a longer passage than this. If you'd gone on to look at the whole scene, you might have mentioned Cleopatra's response, which is against expectations, and sharp, shown by her language: 'Nay, and most like', beginning her presentation as either a 'wrangling Queen' or of 'infinite variety'. Antony's language is heightened and noble, while indicating the enormity of his treachery to Rome's ideals: 'Let Rome in Tiber melt'. The idea of falling is present, too, and that of punishment for these attitudes. Antony's diction is full of the values represented by Egypt in the play: 'the love of Love', 'her soft hours', 'pleasure', 'sport'. 'Speak not to us' is a dramatic and dismissive exit line, leaving Roman disapproval centre stage again, with a sense of a declined and changed leader who is 'not Antony' – a failed ideal.

Now read these extracts from Act 5 Scene 3 of *Richard III* and work through Activity 10 that follows.

EXTRACT 1

[*Enter, to his tent,* KING RICHARD III, NORFOLK, RATCLIFF, CATESBY, *and others.*]

KING RICHARD III   What is't o'clock?

CATESBY   It's supper-time, my lord;
It's nine o'clock.

KING RICHARD III   I will not sup to-night.
Give me some ink and paper.
What, is my beaver easier than it was?
And all my armour laid into my tent?

CATESBY   It is, my liege; and all things are in readiness.   10

KING RICHARD III   Good Norfolk, hie thee to thy charge;
Use careful watch, choose trusty sentinels.

NORFOLK   I go, my lord.

KING RICHARD III   Stir with the lark to-morrow, gentle Norfolk.

NORFOLK   I warrant you, my lord.

[*Exit.*]

KING RICHARD III	Catesby!
CATESBY	My lord?
KING RICHARD III	Send out a pursuivant at arms

To Stanley's regiment; bid him bring his power   20
Before sunrising, lest his son George fall
Into the blind cave of eternal night.

[*Exit* CATESBY.]

Fill me a bowl of wine. Give me a watch.
Saddle white Surrey for the field to-morrow.
Look that my staves be sound, and not too heavy.
Ratcliff!

RATCLIFF	My lord?
KING RICHARD III	Saw'st thou the melancholy Lord Northumberland?
RATCLIFF	Thomas the Earl of Surrey, and himself, 30

Much about cock-shut time, from troop to troop
Went through the army, cheering up the soldiers.

KING RICHARD III So, I am satisfied. Give me a bowl of wine:
I have not that alacrity of spirit,
Nor cheer of mind, that I was wont to have.
Set it down. Is ink and paper ready?

RATCLIFF	It is, my lord.
KING RICHARD III	Bid my guard watch; leave me.

Ratcliff, about the mid of night come to my tent
And help to arm me. Leave me, I say.   40

[*Exeunt* RATCLIFF *and the other* ATTENDANTS.]

EXTRACT 2

RICHMOND   Once more, good night, kind lords and gentlemen.

[*Exeunt all but* RICHMOND.]

O Thou, whose captain I account myself,
Look on my forces with a gracious eye;
Put in their hands thy bruising irons of wrath,
That they may crush down with a heavy fall
The usurping helmets of our adversaries!
Make us thy ministers of chastisement,
That we may praise thee in the victory!
To thee I do commend my watchful soul,   10
Ere I let fall the windows of mine eyes:
Sleeping and waking, O, defend me still!

[*Sleeps.*]

ACTIVITY 10

This passage takes place at Bosworth Field, before the battle which is to end the play, and Richard's life. Look for features of form, structure and language, including the way that characters are presented, dramatic effects, and the central ideas of the play, using the following questions to help you.

1 What is Richard's attitude to his lords and followers here? Is it the same throughout this relatively short passage, or does it seem to change? How?

2 What can you infer from their words about the lords' attitudes to Richard?

3 What is Richmond's attitude to his 'lords and gentlemen'?

4 Look carefully at the sentence forms, and the lengths of sentences, used by Shakespeare to show Richard's state of mind, and Richmond's. What conclusions can you draw about the moods of each of them, and the difference between them?

5 Look carefully at the rhythm of Richard's lines, and those of Richmond. Which seems more regular? Find examples to support your answer. What does this show about their states of mind?

6 Compare the attitudes of Richard and Richmond to God. What do their attitudes show about them?

Looking at a scene in the context of the whole play

Some of the ideas which may be useful to you in considering how to tackle this sort of task are dealt with in 'Looking at part of the text', in the coursework suggestions on page ooo. An exam question might ask you to see the scene in relation to the rest of the play in some way, showing how details relate to descriptions elsewhere, or the significance of this particular scene. The passage below, and the commentary on it, show you the sort of things you need to be thinking about. You'll always be asked to discuss form, structure and language, dramatic features, and the writer's meanings, so the focus in the commentary is on the skill of making comparisons with the rest of the play.

This passage is from *The Tempest*, Act 3 Scene 3:

> [*Thunder and lightning. Enter* ARIEL, *like a Harpy; claps his wings upon the table; and, with a quaint device, the banquet vanishes.*]

ARIEL   You are three men of sin, whom Destiny,
That hath to instrument this lower world
And what is in't, the never-surfeited sea
Hath caused to belch up you; and on this island
Where man doth not inhabit; you 'mongst men

Being most unfit to live. I have made you mad;
And even with such-like valour men hang and drown   10
Their proper selves.

[ALONSO, SEBASTIAN *and c. draw their swords.*]

You fools! I and my fellows
Are ministers of Fate: the elements,
Of whom your swords are temper'd, may as well
Wound the loud winds, or with bemock'd-at stabs
Kill the still-closing waters, as diminish
One dowle that's in my plume: my fellow-ministers
Are like invulnerable. If you could hurt,
Your swords are now too massy for your strengths   20
And will not be uplifted. But remember –
For that's my business to you – that you three
From Milan did supplant good Prospero;
Exposed unto the sea, which hath requit it,
Him and his innocent child: for which foul deed
The powers, delaying, not forgetting, have
Incensed the seas and shores, yea, all the creatures,
Against your peace. Thee of thy son, Alonso,
They have bereft; and do pronounce by me:
Lingering perdition, worse than any death   30
Can be at once, shall step by step attend
You and your ways; whose wraths to guard you from –
Which here, in this most desolate isle, else falls
Upon your heads – is nothing but heart-sorrow
And a clear life ensuing.

[*He vanishes in thunder; then, to soft music enter the* SHAPES
*again, and dance, with mocks and mows, and carrying out
the table.*]

PROSPERO   Bravely the figure of this harpy hast thou
Perform'd, my Ariel; a grace it had, devouring: 40
Of my instruction hast thou nothing bated
In what thou hadst to say: so, with good life
And observation strange, my meaner ministers
Their several kinds have done. My high charms work
And these mine enemies are all knit up
In their distractions; they now are in my power;
And in these fits I leave them, while I visit
Young Ferdinand, whom they suppose is drown'd,
And his and mine loved darling.

[*Exit above.*]   50

GONZALO	I' the name of something holy, sir, why stand you In this strange stare?
ALONSO	O, it is monstrous, monstrous: Methought the billows spoke and told me of it; The winds did sing it to me, and the thunder, That deep and dreadful organ-pipe, pronounced The name of Prosper: it did bass my trespass. Therefore my son i' the ooze is bedded, and I'll seek him deeper than e'er plummet sounded And with him there lie mudded. 60
	[*Exit.*]
SEBASTIAN	But one fiend at a time, I'll fight their legions o'er.
ANTONIO	I'll be thy second.
	[*Exeunt* SEBASTIAN, *and* ANTONIO.]
GONZALO	All three of them are desperate: their great guilt, Like poison given to work a great time after, Now 'gins to bite the spirits. I do beseech you That are of suppler joints, follow them swiftly And hinder them from what this ecstasy 70 May now provoke them to.

The appearance of Ariel here is one of the most dramatic moments in the play, the effect increased by the contrast with the strange beauty of the magical scene immediately preceding it, and the sudden transition to 'thunder and lightning' and the appearance of the harpy. The audience may well be reminded of the tempest at the beginning of the play. This time, however, they know that Prospero has created the storm. The change to 'soft music within the scene prefigures the end, when Prospero asks the audience themselves for 'gentle breath' to drive him home. Magic as part of dramatic form runs through the play, as does music; the two come together in the masque in Act 4. The music is referred to in imagery, too – the winds 'sing' and the thunder is an 'organ-pipe', perhaps reminding the audience of Ariel's visitation to Ferdinand, and the music 'i'th'air'.

This is a central moment in the structure of the play, in several ways. It is a key moment in the play; this is the first time that this group feel Prospero's power, and their reactions are the key to what will happen in the rest of the play. It is a key moment in Prospero's plot, too; his 'enemies' are 'in my power'. Alonso learns of his son's death here, and the combined effect of this and the name of 'Prosper' sends him to the sea. His threat to drown himself may well remind the audience of Ariel's song 'Full fathom five thy father lies' – it seems to be about to come true – but with it the possibility of a 'sea-change'. It is penitence that will bring about this change, and this is signalled for the first time here – forgiveness lies in cure by 'heart-sorrow/And a clear life ensuing'. When this is expressed to Prospero in Act 5, it sparks the revelation which he already knows – Ferdinand is alive. It is also interesting to note that at this point, with two-thirds of the play gone and the finale to come, the playwright chooses to remind the audience of the key bits of plot – the casting out to sea of Prospero and Miranda, and the fact that Ferdinand is still alive.

The language of religion is evident in this passage, as elsewhere in the play. 'You are three men of sin' is a clear moral condemnation, as is the 'trespass' that Alonso accuses himself of. 'Ling'ring perdition' is threatened by Ariel, but after the action of 'heart-sorrow' the end of the play is dominated by 'blessings' and 'grace', mentioned by Prospero here. The invocation 'Heavens rain grace on that which breeds between 'em' has already been pronounced by Prospero on Miranda and Ferdinand, prefiguring the end of the play, when even Caliban 'seeks for grace'. A contrast is formed between the 'innocent child' and the 'foul deed' that threatens it. The other 'innocent' in the play is the oldest character, Gonzalo, whose innocence is seen as 'holy'. 'I'th'name of some thing holy' marks this, as does Prospero directly in Act 4, referring to him as 'holy Gonzalo'. Gonzalo assumes that for all three 'men of sin' their 'great guilt' is now beginning to 'bite the spirits'. He is too optimistic, of course: only one of the three shows clear evidence of feeling guilt, and preparing for change.

Ariel's language is full of threat – the men of sin are 'unfit to live', the powers are 'delaying, not forgetting', and the seas and shores are 'incens'd'. By Act 5, this has changed – 'though the seas threaten, they are merciful'. In this passage the waters are 'still-closing', and potentially the agent of Alonso's drowning; at the end of the play 'calm seas' are promised. At the end of the play those who are capable of change, including, perhaps, Prospero himself, have found their 'proper selves' – mentioned here, and by Gonzalo in Act 5, when he says that 'all of us (found) ourselves/When no man was his own'. 'Fate', 'the powers', and most directly the power of Prospero, through Ariel, seem threatening and dangerous to the characters here, and perhaps to the audience – but the signs are here too that prepare for the 'wonder' and 'miracle' of Act 5.

Comparing two extracts

Another possible style of question is a comparison of two shorter passages, perhaps asking you to look at change or development between the two. Form/structure/language, dramatic effects, and independent opinion and judgement still need to be dealt with, however.

Overleaf is an example of how this sort of task might be approached, using two extracts from *The Taming of the Shrew*, the first from Act 3 Scene 2 and the second from Act 5 Scene 2:

EXTRACT 1

KATHARINA	Nay, then,
	Do what thou canst, I will not go to-day;
	No, nor to-morrow, nor till I please myself.
	The door is open, sir, there lies your way;
	You may be jogging whiles your boots are green;
	For me, I'll not be gone till I please myself.
	'Tis like you'll prove a jolly surly groom,
	That take it on you at the first so roundly.
PETRUCHIO	O Kate! content thee: prithee, be not angry.
KATHARINA	I will be angry: what hast thou to do?
	Father, be quiet; he shall stay my leisure.
GRUMIO	Ay, marry, sir, now it begins to work.
KATHARINA	Gentlemen, forward to the bridal dinner:
	I see a woman may be made a fool,
	If she had not a spirit to resist.
PETRUCHIO	They shall go forward, Kate, at thy command.
	Obey the bride, you that attend on her;
	Go to the feast, revel and domineer,
	Carouse full measure to her maidenhead,
	Be mad and merry, or go hang yourselves:
	But for my bonny Kate, she must with me.
	Nay, look not big, nor stamp, nor stare, nor fret;
	I will be master of what is mine own:
	She is my goods, my chattels; she is my house,
	My household stuff, my field, my barn,
	My horse, my ox, my ass, my anything;
	And here she stands, touch her whoever dare;
	I'll bring mine action on the proudest he
	That stops my way in Padua. Grumio,
	Draw forth thy weapon, we are beset with thieves;
	Rescue thy mistress, if thou be a man.
	Fear not, sweet wench, they shall not touch thee, Kate:
	I'll buckler thee against a million.

Line numbers: 10, 20, 30

[*Exeunt* PETRUCHIO, KATHARINA, *and* GRUMIO.]

The task is to consider the alterations in Kate's feelings, and in the relationship between the two central characters, and to consider the dramatic effects of the two passages.

You would begin, probably, by looking carefully at the first passage. There are several *language* features in Kate's speeches here which present her feelings. From 'Nay then' her words are full of negatives – what she will not do. There are six examples in the first eight lines. The syntax is simple and direct, as in 'For me, I'll not be gone till I please myself', and this is reinforced by form: she has twelve lines here, and eight of them are **end-stopped**, making her speech very blunt and clear. Of the eight sentences, five are statements (though 'there lies your way' makes one of them nearly a command), two are commands, to her father and the 'Gentlemen', and one is a rhetorical question. There is no doubt here. She has little time for men: 'groom', father, gentlemen are to be dismissed and commanded, and 'a woman' must have 'a spirit to resist'. Her husband, certainly, cannot command her: 'What hast thou to do?'

Petruchio, typically and cleverly, turns Kate's words against her. He pretends to agree with her, and commands 'Obey the bride', before inventing an imaginary protest from the company. His language is as plain and strong as hers – 'I will be', 'she is' – and even more commanding. There are eight commands in his speech at the end of the extract, and again form underlines the decisiveness: in 'I will be' and 'She is' the stress falls on the second syllable, and in the imperative 'she must with me' it is the modal verb and the pronoun that are stressed. Lists are used twice to emphasise determination and ownership. 'Big', 'stamp', 'stare', and 'fret' are all emphasised by the rhythm, as are the items in the last of things which Kate is, according to Petruchio. 'Thing' is the last item, in fact, perhaps chosen to stress not only ownership, already insisted on by the repetition nine times of 'my', but also the equating of Kate to inanimate objects as well as beasts. The list carries biblical echoes, too, perhaps to suggest further the patriarchal attitude. Kate has not yet learnt to conform, so she must be taught a lesson.

Dramatically, the seizure of Kate and her removal, presumably forcibly, are not only strong in terms of stage action, but also **symbolise** Petruchio's control and ownership of her, achieved by physical force. The dramatic centre of the passage, though, is when Petruchio starts to speak at 'They shall go forward', where the conflict between them is addressed directly. It is noticeable that Kate does not speak again before she is removed – perhaps she is prevented from doing so?

Now look at the second passage, and start to look for differences. Working through Activity 11 that follows should help you to explore the contrasts in detail.

EXTRACT 2

KATHARINA   Fie, fie! unknit that threatening unkind brow,
             And dart not scornful glances from those eyes,
             To wound thy lord, thy king, thy governor:
             It blots thy beauty as frosts do bite the meads,
             Confounds thy fame as whirlwinds shake fair buds,
             And in no sense is meet or amiable.
             A woman mov'd is like a fountain troubled,
             Muddy, ill-seeming, thick, bereft of beauty;
             And while it is so, none so dry or thirsty
             Will deign to sip or touch one drop of it.   10
             Thy husband is thy lord, thy life, thy keeper,

Thy head, thy sovereign; one that cares for thee,
And for thy maintenance commits his body
To painful labour both by sea and land,
To watch the night in storms, the day in cold,
Whilst thou liest warm at home, secure and safe;
And craves no other tribute at thy hands
But love, fair looks and true obedience;
Too little payment for so great a debt.
Such duty as the subject owes the prince,   20
Even such a woman oweth to her husband;
And when she is froward, peevish, sullen, sour,
And not obedient to his honest will,
What is she but a foul contending rebel,
And graceless traitor to her loving lord? –
I am asham'd that women are so simple
To offer war where they should kneel for peace,
Or seek for rule, supremacy, and sway,
When they are bound to serve, love, and obey.
Why are our bodies soft, and weak, and smooth,   30
Unapt to toil and trouble in the world,
But that our soft conditions and our hearts
Should well agree with our external parts?
Come, come, you froward and unable worms!
My mind hath been as big as one of yours,
My heart as great, my reason haply more,
To bandy word for word and frown for frown;
But now I see our lances are but straws,
Our strength as weak, our weakness past compare,
That seeming to be most which we indeed least are.   40
Then vail your stomachs, for it is no boot,
And place your hands below your husband's foot:
In token of which duty, if he please,
My hand is ready; may it do him ease.

PETRUCHIO   Why, there's a wench! Come on, and kiss me, Kate.

LUCENTIO   Well, go thy ways, old lad, for thou shalt ha't.

VINCENTO   'Tis a good hearing when children are toward.

LUCENTIO   But a harsh hearing when women are froward.

PETRUCHIO   Come, Kate, we'll to bed.
              We three are married, but you two are sped ...   50

ACTIVITY 11

1 Kate's language is quite different here. Look carefully at the length and complexity of the sentences, and the number of end-stopped lines. Look at statements, commands and questions too, and notice who is being commanded, in contrast to the first passage. Notice the structures she uses, which build item after item in a very controlled, almost formal way. Look back to the first passage again, to find a clear contrast to use as evidence.

2 There are no rhyming couplets in the first passage. Check this second passage for rhymes, and their frequency. Why should there be rhymes here, and not in the first?

3 Kate's attitude to men, and to husbands, seems to have changed completely. What do the lists beginning 'thy lord' remind you of in the first passage – and who was speaking then? What might this linguistic choice be suggesting about the change in Kate?

4 Look through the speech for all the words referring to men. Notice how many of them suggest ruling.

5 Some of Kate's language suggests war being waged by women, where 'they should kneel for peace'. Find these words, and consider what they imply about men, and about women.

6 Look at what Kate suggests about the nature of women, and the various ways in which she suggests that they are weak.

7 Kate's closing words form a dramatic gesture. Silence is also dramatic, though. Petruchio says very little here, compared to his volubility in the rest of the play. What is the significance of this?

8 There are a number of ways you might interpret Kate's apparent capitulation to Petruchio, which is certainly uncomfortable for a modern audience. Perhaps she is being ironic throughout, even to the extent of using Petruchio's linguistic terms and structures. Do the men really have the power here? Nevertheless, Petruchio seems to be the winner in several senses. Your response to the ending, which the comparison invites you to make, will clearly enable you to form an *independent opinion and judgement*, informed by *knowledge and understanding*, and taking into account the ways in which Shakespeare's uses of *form, structure and language shape meanings*. In other words, you can address all the relevant Assessment Objectives.

Presentation of an idea or a character

An examination question might ask you to respond to the ways Shakespeare presents an idea in the play, or a character. 'How you respond to …' or 'What do you find interesting about …' are examples of phrases which invite you to address AO4, '*articulate independent opinions and judgements*', and 'presentation' invites AO3, '*the ways in which writers' choices of form, structure and language shape meanings*'.

An example of the ways you might think about a question about an idea is given in the Coursework section, under 'Offering an interpretation' (page 66). In the examination, the question might be phrased 'How do you respond to the presentation of women in the play?', but your process and the range of material you might use would be the same.

If you decide to choose an examination task which focuses on a character, you must be very careful not to simply write about the character in the play as if he or she were a real person, rather than a character in a play presented by a writer in particular ways, with particular purposes within a dramatic construct. You must remember, in other words, the Assessment Objectives.

If you were studying *Richard III*, you could be asked, 'What do you find interesting about the presentation of Richard in the play?' Working through the questions below will remind you of the sort of features you might deal with in shaping your response.

ACTIVITY 12

The questions below are grouped according to structure, language and form, as these are the elements you need to think about.

Structure

1   How does Richard dominate the play? Think about the opening and the ending of the play. What effect might this dominance have on the audience? What happens when he is not on the stage?

2   How does the presentation of Richard change after he has gained the throne? Think about the scenes with Anne in the first half of the play, and Elizabeth in the second. How is Richard different?

Language

3   How is Richard described, by himself and by others? Think about the animal imagery, for instance.

4   What are Richard's attitudes to women, and how are they expressed? Think about what he says about them, and what he says when he is with them.

5   What are Richard's attitudes to his followers, and how are they expressed, in words and actions?

6   What is Richard's attitude to God, and to conscience, and how are his attitudes expressed?

Form

7   What do you think Richard's relationship with the audience is? How do the audience know more of his thoughts than those of any other character?

8   How does Shakespeare use minor characters to make the audience reflect on Richard? Think about the way children are used, for example.

9 How does Shakespeare use ghosts to give the audience a sense of Richard's fate?

10 How does Shakespeare use punctuation and changes in metre to show Richard's moods?

This gives you a wide range of material to use, and covers each of the elements of Assessment Objective 3. You still have to build into your response AO4, however – you have to respond to 'What did you find interesting about … ?' This should inform your whole response, from the beginning. Do not simply pay lip service to this by repeating it all the time. What did you actually find interesting about some of the issues raised above, or any others? It is your reasoned individual response that the examiner is looking for, and will reward.

Activity 12 concentrates on *Richard III.* but of course this approach is equally valuable for any text that you might be studying for this unit. The suggestions and activities given in this exam option section are not meant to be exhaustive. They are examples of the sort of tasks you might be set, and the ways in which you must pay attention to the Assessment Objectives in responding to them.

Module ③ Texts in Context – Drama and Poetry

This module carries 40% of the total marks for the AS level course.
The marks are divided amongst the Assessment Objectives like this:

ASSESSMENT OBJECTIVES

AO1   communicate clearly the knowledge, understanding and insight appropriate to literary study, using appropriate terminology and accurate and coherent written expression
(5% of the final AS mark; 2.5% of the final A level mark)

AO2i   respond with knowledge and understanding to literary texts of different types and periods
(5% of the final AS mark; 2.5% of the final A level mark)

AO3   show detailed understanding of the ways in which writers' choices of form, structure and language shape meanings
(5% of the final AS mark; 2.5% of the final A level mark)

AO4   articulate independent opinions and judgements informed by different interpretations of literary texts by other readers
(10% of the final AS mark; 5% of the final A level mark)

AO5i   show understanding of the contexts in which literary texts are written and understood.
(15% of the final AS mark; 7.5% of the final A level mark)

All the Assessment Objectives are tested in this module, and they are allocated to period in the following way:

Pre 1900 Drama and Poetry
Assessment Objective 1
Assessment Objective 2i – split between both sections
Assessment Objective 3
Assessment Objective 5i – the dominant objective worth 15% of the marks

Post 1900 Drama and Poetry
Assessment Objective 1
Assessment Objective 2i – split between both sections
Assessment Objective 3
Assessment Objective 4 – the dominant objective worth 10% of the marks

The main emphasis for your studies will be the dominant Assessment Objective for each period, although it is necessary to pay attention to the other objectives as well.

Content

This module meets the syllabus requirements for drama and poetry. It also meets the Pre 1900 period requirement.

The structure of the module

Module 3 is spit into two sections: Section A Drama and Section B Poetry. Each section is then sub-divided by period into Pre 1900 and Post 1900.

The examination

The question paper is split into two sections, Section A Drama, and Section B Poetry. You will answer one question from each genre, remembering that the two texts *must* be from different periods. You are allowed to take your texts into the examination.

Section A: Drama

Preparing for the Pre 1900 texts

For the Pre 1900 texts you need to address the following Assessment Objectives:

Assessment Objectives 1, 2i, 3, 5i.

Assessment Objectives 1 and 2i will be automatically met as you work through your texts and acquire knowledge, understanding and critical terminology. Assessment Objective 3 will be considered side-by-side with your study of contexts, AO5i, as you will demonstrate how the various contexts are conveyed through the writers' choices of form, structure and language.

Understanding contexts

The examination on the Pre 1900 Drama or the Pre 1900 Poetry in this module are the *only times* that you will be tested on Assessment Objective 5i at AS level. However, there is no need to feel concerned about this objective. In the Introduction you looked at the various types of contexts you need to consider:

- *the context of a period or era, including significant social, historical, political and cultural processes*: you will see that this context will involve the consideration of themes in a way that will probably be familiar from your studies at GCSE.

- *the context of a given or specific passage in terms of the whole work from which it is taken*: this is a part-to-whole context where you would be expected to relate an extract to the whole text.

- *the context of the work in terms of other texts, including other works by the same author*: this will apply to the poetry section where you will consider several poems by the same author.

- *the literary context, including the question of generic factors and period-specific styles*. A genre is a specific kind of writing. At AS level you will look at three different genres, the novel, drama and poetry, exploring the particular characteristics of each type.

What are contexts?

It might be helpful to think about contexts as two sets of frameworks, the outer and the inner frames or contexts related to each text.

A writer may develop a *social context* within the text where there is exploration of aspects of society such as love or marriage, faith or social behaviour and morality. The inner context or frame could also be *political*, with enquiries into political behaviour, or *legal*, with the exploration of matters such as justice. *Historical contexts* could involve issues such as slavery or governmental attitudes. You will soon find that within the frame of reference which the author constructs you are back to the familiar territory of exploring themes or concerns.

The outer contexts would include matters of *genre*, such as the relationship of a Jacobean play to the revenge genre, or of *period*, such as how historical or stylistic matters have affected a particular author.

At AS level the contexts may generally be drawn from within the text itself. Any explanation necessary to 'place' your chosen text in a context external to the text may be given by your teacher, or will be explained in this book. At A2 level you will be expected to explore these outer contexts yourself and relate them to the text. This will be tested in the Coursework, where you will have plenty of help in making sure you achieve the contexts, and also in the Synoptic Unit at the end of the course where you will have opportunity to prepare your ideas before the exam.

You may wonder why contexts are applied only to the Pre 1900 texts. The contexts for these texts are largely those of past times, and are therefore mostly settled and complete, unlike the contexts surrounding modern literature which are still unfolding. Another reason is that because poetry is ambiguous, and rests for its effectiveness on multiple readings, and because modern poetry may be initially more accessible to AS students than Pre 1900 poetry, Ao4, independent opinions/different interpretations of the text, has been applied to the newer texts.

Pre 1900 Drama

The aim of this section is to explore a series of contexts drawn from several plays. You will learn how to compile evidence from a text in order to demonstrate how a particular context becomes evident and acquires significance for your interpretation of the play.

How to explore contexts

Although this section may look at only one or two contexts from particular texts, this does *not* mean that it is the *only* context evident in these texts. This section offers a demonstration of how to explore a particular context as an example of how you should investigate contexts generally. Likewise, do not think that any reading of a play discussed here is the sole reading. Remember that all texts are open to several different readings.

Here are the different types of contexts which will be used as examples of how to cover Assessment Objective 5i:

- contexts of period and genre in the morality play

- the dramatic context of the Renaissance tragic hero

- the theatrical context

- moral contexts

- the biographical context

- the context of love and of family relationships.

The pre 1900 drama in this module is drawn from three main periods or types: Elizabethan, Revenge Tragedy and the New Drama, Social Comedy.

Elizabethan drama – *Dr Faustus* by Christopher Marlowe

AO5i: The two contexts to be explored are:

1 *Dr Faustus* as a morality play: the contexts of period and of genre.

2 Faustus himself in the context of the *Elizabethan tragic hero*, which involves the contexts of period and genre.

Remember that there are other readings possible within these contexts, and that there are other readings of the text overall. For the purposes of this example, we will consider a Christian reading, but this is not the only interpretation of this play.

AO2i: knowledge and understanding of the text

In *Dr Faustus* Marlowe may, in one interpretation, be seen to explore the Elizabethan celebration of the achievement of Renaissance man. But at the same time he explores the darker aspects of Faustus's pride, which leads to sin and damnation.

In the play, Faustus makes a pact with the devil: he will surrender his soul on a set date in exchange for skills in the magic art of necromancy. Necromancy is the art of predicting the future by means of communication with the dead, a sort of black magic. In Christian terms, knowledge of the future belongs only to God. So, in one interpretation of the play, Faustus may be seen as wrong in trying to assume this power. He comes to regret his pact with the devil, but despair affects his ability to repent.

AO3/AO5i: how the writer expresses the ideas related to these contexts

---

Dr Faustus as a morality play: the contexts of period and of genre

The morality play was a popular type of drama in the fourteenth and fifteenth centuries. The subject of the plays was man, how he survived temptation and overcame his sins or errors to achieve salvation. There were at least two plays which were significant for later drama and for *Dr Faustus* – *The Castle of Perseverance* and *Everyman*.

A. **Castle of Perseverance** is a late fifteenth-century morality play. Forces representing good and evil were personified in characters on the stage: the Good Angels were the forces of goodness; and characters representing the forces of evil included the Bad Angels, the Devil and the Seven Deadly Sins. (The seven deadly sins according to Christian belief are: pride, covetousness or greed, envy, wrath or anger, gluttony, sloth and lechery or lust.) You will see these characters incorporated into *Dr Faustus*.

B. **Everyman** is another morality play in which a man, representing the whole of mankind, is shown how to overcome temptation to achieve salvation. His great friend is Good Counsel, which means Good Advice, and in *Dr Faustus* this character becomes the Old Man.

What evidence of these morality features is there in *Dr Faustus*?

- At the very beginning of *Dr Faustus*, the Chorus speaks the prologue, which points out the theme of morality to the audience:

> Only this (Gentlemen) we must perform,
> The form of Faustus' fortunes good or bad.
> To patient judgements we appeal our plaud, ...

The Chorus describes Faustus's merits, his rise and his fall.

- The forces of evil are represented on the stage by the Evil Angel, the devils, Lucifer, Mephastophilis, and Belzebub.

- The forces of good are represented by the Good Angel and Old Man.

- When the Good and the Evil Angels appear on stage they are seen trying to persuade Faustus to behave in opposite ways. For example, the first time they appear in Scene 1 Faustus has become interested in necromancy. They each address Faustus:

> GOOD ANGEL   O Faustus, lay that damned book aside,
> And gaze not on it, lest it tempt thy soul
> And heap God's heavy wrath upon thy head: ...
>
> EVIL ANGEL   Go forward, Faustus, in that famous art
> Wherein all nature's treasury is contained.

But there is something more complex going on here than simple persuasion. These angels actually represent Faustus's inner struggle. Whenever these angels appear, you should be aware that they are enacting Faustus's inner thoughts on stage.

ACTIVITY 1

How do you think these speeches suggest what is going on in Faustus's mind? If you are studying this text, work through the play and list the appearances of the Good and the Bad Angels, looking at who speaks first and why, and then work out what Faustus is thinking and feeling. Here is a second example for you to consider. Faustus realises that Mephastophilis has helped lead him to damnation, and the Angels appear again:

FAUSTUS	'Tis thou has damned distressed Faustus' soul: Is't not too late?
EVIL ANGEL	Too late.
GOOD ANGEL	Never too late, if Faustus can repent.
EVIL ANGEL	If thou repent, devils shall tear thee in pieces.
GOOD ANGEL	Repent, and they shall never rase thy skin.

Can you see the central irony of this exchange? As a Christian, Faustus should remember that Christ has infinite mercy, and his repentance would gain immediate salvation, and 'immunity' from the devils. But Faustus is slipping into the sin of despair, because he is rejecting the central Christian belief in Christ's mercy and the redemption of all who plead to Christ. You can see this sense of hopelessness from the way his mind works here.

- The parade of the Seven Deadly Sins in Scene 5 is also used to show the audience Faustus's inner state of mind, and how he has deteriorated. He has no sense of the evil of the representations on stage, but finds them entertaining. Hence his response to each of them is lighthearted, for example, in his comments to Lechery:

FAUSTUS	And what are you, Mistress Minx, the seventh and last?

- The character of the Old Man is the equivalent of Good Counsel in *Everyman*. He tries hard to save Faustus from hell in Scene 12:

OLD MAN	Ah Doctor Faustus, that I might prevail To guide thy steps unto the way of life, By which sweet path thou may'st attain the goal That shall conduct thee to celestial rest.

But it is too late because, as you have seen, Faustus has given in to despair, ironically a by-product of his pride, one of the Seven Deadly Sins which he had laughed at earlier. Faustus now does not believe that God could forgive him, so he is destined for hell. The Old Man realises this:

> OLD MAN   Accursed Faustus, miserable man,
> That from thy soul exclud'st the grace of heaven,
> And fliest the throne of His tribunal seat!

- The Chorus concludes the play with an epilogue to sum it all up:

> CHORUS   Cut is the branch that might have grown full straight,
> And burned is Apollo's laurel bough …
> Faustus is gone! Regard his hellish fall, …

As you have seen, Marlowe has incorporated at least seven elements of the older morality play into *Dr Faustus*:

- the Chorus who spells out the moral of the play

- the forces of evil represented on stage

- the forces of good, the angel and the Old Man represented on stage

- the Good and the Evil Angels enacting Faustus's inner struggle

- the Seven Deadly Sins revealing Faustus's inner state of mind

- the Old Man as a giver of good advice

- the Chorus's epilogue used to summarise events.

Remember that this is only one Christian reading of the play related to this context; the final Chorus's speech is ambiguous, and could be a warning about falling into the same position as Faustus, who could not repent because of seeing things only one way. Likewise, you could regard the Old Man, or even the Good Angel, as less than useful to Faustus because they have taken only one view of his actions, and presume that the doctor is past help, or is finally damned. In a non-Christian reading of the text, for example, the evidence would be assembled differently, and Faustus's death would be seen in other ways.

Faustus as Elizabethan tragic hero

Two types of contexts can be seen in this interpretation:

1 Elizabethan man as a tragic hero, within the social/historical context of the period in which the play was written

2 exploration of Faustus as a tragic hero in the context of dramatic genre.

There are certain characteristics of Faustus which you could examine here:

- He has achieved some status with his studies, but still feels somehow unfulfilled.

- He is ambitious and proud of what he has done, but seems to be bored.

- He achieves through necromancy what he set out to do, but the consequences are not what he had imagined.

- He realises his plan has failed and is thrown into confusion, disappointment, and perhaps despair.

His status

Faustus's very first speech reveals a lot about his status and his achievements, ambitions and frustrations:

> FAUSTUS   Settle thy studies, Faustus, and begin
> To sound the depth of that thou wilt profess:
> Having commenced, be a divine in show,
> Yet level at the end of every art,
> And live and die in Aristotle's works. …
> Is, to dispute well, logic's chiefest end?
> Affords this art no greater miracle?
> Then read no more, thou hast attained the end;
> A greater subject fitteth Faustus' wit.

ACTIVITY 2

You can see that already Dr Faustus had achieved much, but wants to go much further. How does Marlowe convey these ideas in this speech?

His ambitions

Even at the end of the first speech, Faustus is beginning to change his attitude towards magic and necromancy:

> O what a world of profit and delight,
> Of power, of honour, of omnipotence
> Is promised to the studious artisan!

Later, in Scene 3, Faustus has practised magic and believes that he has called up Mephastophilis:

FAUSTUS	Did not he charge thee to appear to me?
MEPHASTOPHILIS	No, I came now hither of mine own accord.
FAUSTUS	Did not my conjuring speeches raise thee? Speak!

Although Mephastophilis explains that it was coincidence, Faustus will not listen to him, choosing to believe that his own new powers have worked.

ACTIVITY 3

1 Looking at both of these short speeches above, work out what you think Faustus's weaknesses are so far.

2 Try to pinpoint the ways in which his character has already begun to change.

Consequences of his decisions and actions

Even when Faustus is writing the pact and his blood congeals so that he cannot sign his name at first in Scene 5, he ignores the warning, and with this the chance to prevent his fall:

| FAUSTUS | What might the staying of my blood portend?
 Is it unwilling I should write this bill? |

ACTIVITY 4

Make a list of all the things that Faustus tells Mephastophilis that he wants.

The comic middle scenes of the play reveal to the audience just how little Faustus has achieved: Mephastophilis could not supply Faustus with any real knowledge, although they do time-travel together. Generally, you are made to see the pettiness of Faustus's new powers. He becomes a pathetic practical joker, conjuring little magic tricks for kings and dukes: tricking a horse-dealer and heckling the Pope. For example, Faustus is made invisible by Mephastophilis in Scene 7:

MEPHASTOPHILIS	So Faustus, now do what thou wilt, thou shall not be discerned.
POPE	My lord of Lorraine, will't please you draw near.
FAUSTUS	Fall to; and the devil choke you and you spare.

This use of comic scenes is evident in much of Elizabethan and Jacobean drama and can be seen as a type of *generic context*. Such scenes have several purposes, including:

- amusing the audience

- developing the ideas in the main plot by enriching the themes, juxtaposing ideas, or turning the action of the main plot upside down.

ACTIVITY 5

Discuss what you think Marlowe is trying to achieve in these comic scenes. What does Faustus seem to achieve by his damnation?

ACTIVITY 6

1 What do you realise about Faustus's character now?

2 Look at his language again. Why do you think that he is made to speak in plain prose instead of the powerful poetry of earlier scenes?

3 How have some of his grand plans and hopes been reversed?

The audience has become aware before Faustus that he has achieved very little. This is called dramatic irony. As the realisation dawns, we see him in his final speech in Scene 13 in mental agony:

> FAUSTUS   Ah Faustus,
> Now hast thou but one bare hour to live,
> And then thou must be damned perpetually. …
> The stars move still, time runs, the clock will strike,
> The devil will come, and Faustus must be damned.
> O I'll leap up to my God! Who pulls me down?
> See, see where Christ's blood streams in the firmament!
> One drop would save my soul, half a drop: ah my Christ – …
> No Faustus, curse thyself, curse Lucifer,
> That hath deprived thee of the joys of heaven.

ACTIVITY 7

Faustus now recognises all that has happened. Write about the ways in which Marlowe portrays this recognition. You need to consider:

- the poetry of the language, the different registers and images

- the ways in which Faustus shows that he understands what has happened

- the ways in which you may think that he still does not understand.

Examine your response to Faustus. Do you feel any sympathy for him now?

(Remember that the scene is discussed in terms of a Christian reading of the play.)

There is an additional scene to this play presented in the Appendix to Text A, Scene 13, but in the main play of Text B. It offers scope for some interesting ideas. After the Chorus's final speech, the scholars come on stage to describe Faustus's ghastly, grisly death. They are totally bewildered:

FIRST SCHOLAR	Come gentlemen, let us go visit Faustus,
	For such a dreadful night was never seen
	Since first the world's creation did begin.
	Such fearful shrieks and cries were never heard!
	Pray heaven the doctor have escaped the danger.
SECOND SCHOLAR	O help us heaven! See, here are Faustus' limbs,
	All torn asunder by the hand of death.

These lines have been used by critics to offer some unusual and contentious readings of the play, supported by the fact that Marlowe himself was reported to have expressed atheistic views, for example in his comment that 'the only end of religion is to keep men in awe'.

The words 'was never seen' and 'were never heard' raise several issues related to various contexts of the play. Marlowe was extremely careful in constructing his verse, so the ambiguity here may well have been deliberate, suggesting at least three possibilities:

1 The idea that such a dreadful night was never seen before. This idea ties in with the traditional readings of the play which you have explored, in the *moral context* of a Christian play.

2 The idea that such a night was *never* seen. With the stress on 'never' the scholars would be seen to suggest that the final events of the play where Faustus is dragged to Hell did not actually happen. What actually occurred was the development of a fantasy in Faustus's mind; so the author offers a psychological study of a deranged mind culminating in a horrible, self-mutilating suicide. This reading offers a *psychological context*.

3 Or Marlowe, through the scholars, could have been addressing the audience, reminding them that what they have seen is just a play, a drama; such a night was actually never seen, as it happened solely on stage. So this reading forms part of the *dramatic context* of the play. Shakespeare uses this technique, for example, at the end of *A Midsummer Night's Dream,* when Puck says to the audience 'you have but slumb'red here'. This is a deliberate

trick of **alienation**, of distancing the audience from what has been performed, and bringing them back to reality to think about whether there may be a moral to be drawn from the entertaining presentation of the play. It is up to you, the individual reader, to make your own decisions about the significance of this drama.

ACTIVITY 8

Finally you could think about the scholars, where there is a very clear ambiguity. You might consider:

- What sort of scholars are they? Are we given a clue?

- Might the study be that of divinity? Or of necromancy? Or of anatomy?

- Could it be another sort of study?

Of course you are free to reject any of these ideas, but since the claims rest on ambiguity, they cannot be either proved or disproved. However, this sort of enquiry always extends your understanding of the play and its possible readings and contexts.

This concludes the exploration of Dr Faustus; hopefully the range of the play will have been impressed on your memory, with the mood changes from frightening diabolical experiences, to slapstick humour. As you have seen, there are several interesting contexts attached to this play, to which you may add several of your own ideas.

Jacobean drama, Revenge Tragedy – 'Tis Pity She's a Whore by John Ford

'Tis Pity She's a Whore belongs to the genre of Revenge Tragedies. This genre is generally considered to have begun in England in 1592, six years after John Ford was born, with the publication of a play called *A Spanish Tragedy,* written by Thomas Kyd. It is also generally accepted that the publication of *'Tis Pity She's a Whore* in 1633 marks the end of this tradition.

AO2i: knowledge and understanding of the text

Revenge plays are, as the name suggests, dramas centred around revenge by one or more of the characters, so understanding this idea of revenge is central to your grasp of this play. You will also need to think about the issue of morality, and whether John Ford has a serious moral purpose in a play which celebrates the spiritual beauty of incestuous love, love between a brother and sister. Critics are divided about this, some believing that he raises serious questions about spirituality and religion, while others maintain that he doesn't care about morality, but is interested in sensational ideas and some sensational effects.

> **Ao5i: show understanding of the contexts in which literary texts are written and understood**

Following on from consideration of Ao2i, the two contexts to be considered at some length are:

- the literary context of *'Tis Pity She's a Whore* as a Revenge Tragedy

- the moral context, an enquiry into the relationship between the spiritual force of incestuous love, and established religious attitudes evident in this play.

(Remember that these are just two of the several contexts and readings you can find in this text.)

> **AO3: how the writer expresses ideas related to these contexts**

The literary context of *'Tis Pity She's a Whore* as Revenge Tragedy

In Elizabethan England the idea of seeking revenge by murder was rather complicated. Whilst the law forbade murder, there was generally a feeling of acceptance and sympathy for a person who sought to gain revenge for the murder of a blood relative or somebody close, such as a wife. This sympathy was shared by the playwrights who often explored the conflict between formal law and 'natural' law in their plays. With this in mind, you might consider the characteristics of Revenge Tragedy:

- there will be one or more revengers

- there is usually an Italian or Spanish setting

- there is intrigue and plotting, violence, and murder

- there is the use of disguise to help bring about the plans for revenge.

ACTIVITY 9

Work through all the features above, and make notes to show how *each* characteristic is evident in this play. Here are some points to help you:

1 List all the revengers, and their motives for revenge; you should include Hippolita, Richardetto, Donado, Grimaldi, Vasquez, Soranzo and even Giovanni. You will find variations on the idea of revenger. Look, for example, at Soranzo's revenge: has he got a motive justifiable by law or 'natural' law? Or is it a less honourable motive?

2 Why does Vasquez say to Soranzo: 'Now you begin to turn Italian'?

3 Think of the central death, that of Annabella: how is her murder linked to the idea of revenge?

4 When you think of disguise, think of actual disguise and why this is necessary for the plotters. But think also of metaphorical disguise, of people not being what they seem to be, such as the lovers, or the Cardinal, and think about what this might suggest about the themes of the play.

The moral context

Some readers believe that John Ford proposes a moral challenge: that unlawful love may be deadly, but it is none the less real and beautiful for that. Do you think that there may be a suggestion that such a love offers more spiritual reward than the perhaps dubious values and teachings of traditional Christianity?

You may focus on six aspects in looking at this context:

- the relationship between Giovanni and Annabella

- the attitudes and behaviour of the Friar

- the attitudes and behaviour of the Cardinal

- the idea of fate

- the sordidness of the other lovers

- the evidence for a moral and Christian frame within the play.

The relationship between Giovanni and Annabella

Look at some of Giovanni's language when he woos Annabella in Act 1 Scene 2:

The lily and the rose, most sweetly strange,
Upon your dimpled cheeks do strive for change.
Such lips would tempt a saint; …

ACTIVITY 10

- Why might Giovanni compare Annabella to flowers?

- Do you find the language sensual and sexual, or delicate and gentle?

- Why does Giovanni make the reference to the saint?

Then there is the striking moment when the lovers exchange vows, first Annabella:

> On my knees,
> Brother, even by our mother's dust, I charge you,
> Do not betray me to your mirth or hate:
> Love me, or kill me, brother.

Then Giovanni repeats her words, ending 'Love me, or kill me, sister'.

ACTIVITY 11

- Is the tone in this extract similar in its quietness? Perhaps understated?

- Why are the words 'sister' and 'brother' spoken? What effect is created?

Finally, look at Giovanni's words later in the play when he thinks about his love:

> O, the glory
> Of two united hearts like hers and mine! ...
> My world and all of happiness is here,
> And I'd not change it for the best to come.
> A life of pleasure is Elysium.

ACTIVITY 12

- Look at the contrast between the quiet tone and the depth of feelings here.

- It is suggested that he would swap Heaven for his love. Does this idea show an understanding of the dangers he is facing for love?

- Or does the speech not work for you?

The attitudes and behaviour of the Friar

The Friar's role should be to give spiritual support. How effectively does he do this? Look at his first advice to Giovanni in Act 1 Scene 1:

> Pray for thyself
> At home, whilst I pray for thee here. Away,
> My blessing with thee. We have need to pray.

In the next Act, he meets Giovanni and realises what has happened:

> Nay, then I see thou'rt too far sold to hell;
> It lies not in the compass of my prayers
> To call thee back. ...

At his final meeting with Giovanni he gives up:

> Go where thou wilt; I see
> The wildness of thy fate draws to an end,
> To a bad, fearful end. I must not stay
> To know thy fall: back to Bologna I ...

ACTIVITY 13

- What sort of support does the Friar offer?

- Is it of any possible help to Giovanni?

- What do you think of the Friar's decision to leave – or flee?

- Is traditional religion any help at all? (You might remember that the Friar's persuasion causes Annabella to marry and leads directly to many deaths.)

The attitudes and behaviour of the Cardinal

The Cardinal is the representative of the head of the Church, and he administers justice as well as religious matters. Hearing Grimaldi confess to the murder of Bergetto he says:

> For this offence I here receive Grimaldi
> Into his Holiness' protection.
> He is no common man, but nobly born ...

Florio retorts 'Justice is fled to Heaven and comes no nearer.'

ACTIVITY 14

- What sort of decision has the Cardinal made here?

- What might it suggest about the morality of the Church?

The idea of fate

Throughout the play Giovanni tries perhaps to bypass his conscience by claiming that his actions were inevitable:

> 'tis my destiny
> That you must either love, or I must die.

There are many such examples, and you must decide how far this might be true, and how far it is convenient for Giovanni to proclaim such an idea.

The sordidness of the other lovers

There are other lovers in the play, but they do not seem to compare well with Giovanni. You should list these, and make brief notes on the way they behave. You should include: the idiotic Bergetto, with his ridiculous letter; the insensitive Grimaldi who thinks that love is a military battle; Soranzo and Hippolita's adulterous affair and his terrifying attitude to Annabella when he discovers that she is pregnant. What effects does a comparison with the love-relationship between Annabella and Giovanni have?

The evidence for a moral and Christian frame within the play

You have already seen above that Giovanni admits he will lose 'Elysium', or heaven, for his love of Annabella. There are many other references to support this frame, for example:

> I carry hell about me; all my blood
> Is fired in swift revenge.

ACTIVITY 15

- Soranzo's words hint that revenge could be linked to hell; might this suggest that the punishment for revenge is to endure hell? How strong is this theme?

- Giovanni often admits to losing hope of heaven, and the Friar says this both to Giovanni and to Annabella. What weight do these references carry?

- Is there any sense of a struggle between religion and love?

In conclusion, it could be said that John Ford seriously and quietly creates an alternative moral and spiritual world which contrasts with and challenges traditional religious thought. Such thought would promote a loveless marriage between Soranzo and Annabella. Traditional religious support in the world of the play is weak or flawed. So John Ford asks you to make a choice: which would you prefer?

(Remember, these are just brief outlines of framework responses. You should extend them in your own time.)

Here are a few more contexts which you might explore in your own time:

The language context: here you might consider the language which the playwright has used. If you explore this context you will touch again upon one of the controversies surrounding this play which you saw earlier. Some critics say that the very plain language suggests the honest and pure feelings of the siblings. Others think that because the language is so plain the play suffers. In earlier great Revenge Tragedies, the author wrote speeches rich in imagery; this meant that references to hell, heaven and divine justice made the audience very aware that the revenger was about to lose his soul. There was also psychological exploration so that the revenger became a type of all revengers. In this play, critics suggest that there is none of this grandness, and that the main characters are finally homely, without great heroic status, just a brother and sister in love.

ACTIVITY 16

Here is an extract from Giovanni's speech in Act 2 Scene 5 when the Friar says that he will visit Annabella:

At your best leisure, father; then she'll tell you
How dearly she doth prize my matchless love.
Then you will know what pity 'twere we two
Should have been sundered from each other's arms.
View well her face, and in that little round
You may observe a world of variety: …

What do you think are the strengths and weaknesses of John Ford's presentation of Giovanni here? How effective is the language? What does this imply about Giovanni?

The dramatic context: how the play works on stage. Here you might think about the relationship between the main plot and the sub-plot, and how they are intertwined; whether the sub-plot characters such as Bergetto and Poggio can be made to appear humorous on stage; the pathos of the scene where Giovanni and Annabella exchange their vows; the clever and fast-paced interweaving of speeches; the dramatic unmasking of Hippolita; the shocking, and maybe sensational appearance of Giovanni appearing with his sister's heart on a dagger.

There is the legal context where you might look at the behaviour of the Cardinal and the citizens of Parma and Italy, and also the Cardinal's decisions.

There is the religious context, which you have touched upon already in the moral context, where you might focus on the attitudes and behaviour of the Friar and the Cardinal.

This concludes your study here of several contexts in the drama *'Tis Pity She's a Whore*. However, there are others which you will go on to explore, perhaps using the models above as a guide. But now it is time to move forward in time to consider a nineteenth-century play.

New Drama: Society Comedy – *A Woman of No Importance* by Oscar Wilde

A Woman of No Importance was first performed in 1895, when Oscar Wilde was at the height of his career as a dramatist. Within four months Wilde was convicted of committing acts of gross indecency in the course of homosexual relationships, and this put an end to his writing of plays.

AO2i: knowledge and understanding of the text

A Woman of No Importance is a type of drama known as Social Comedy, part of the New Drama. New Drama is so-called because from the mid-nineteenth century there was a new concern with issues related to the society of the day, and to the behaviour of members of this society. At this time, theatre-going was a popular social event for the wealthier members of society, who enjoyed seeing plays which were devoted to their own class and their own concerns in great comfort. Obviously, they wished to see a flattering picture of themselves portrayed on stage as certain key social issues were dealt with.

On the surface, Wilde's plays seemed to be typical of social comedies, but below the surface several serious moral issues were considered almost in disguise, because of the elegant humour. In this way, Wilde managed to persuade the audience that he shared and approved of their moral values, but modern readers may find in these plays serious criticism of the society of his age.

AO5i: show understanding of the contexts in which literary texts are written and understood

The three contexts to be considered here are:

- the social context

- the psychological/moral context

- the dramatic context of comedy.

AO3: how the writer expresses ideas related to these contexts

The social context

The social context to be considered here is that of the 'conventional' reading of the play. That is to say, it is a reading which an audience contemporary to the play would find pleasing, as it supports and confirms the social values and attitudes held by this audience.

Since he is the figurehead, and chief representative of the society within the play, the character and role of Lord Illingworth will be explored here.

In Act 3, Lady Hunstanton explains to Mrs Arbuthnot how the 'very brilliant young man about town' came to inherit his title, although he was the younger son. She helps to convey attitudes to Lord Illingworth which are typical responses of the members of this wealthy society.

In Act 1 she congratulates Gerald on being offered the post as secretary to Lord Illingworth, saying: '… That is good news indeed, Gerald. It means a very brilliant future in store for you. …'

Later, the same Lady comments on him:

'I don't know how it is, dear Lord Illingworth, but everything you have said today seems to me excessively immoral. It has been most interesting, listening to you.'

Add to these comments one made by Lady Stutfield about these powerful men in society: 'Men are so very, very heartless.'

ACTIVITY 17

If you look at all these comments together, you will be able to grasp the sort of issues which would interest an audience of the day. You can work these out by thinking about these questions:

- What sort of background is necessary to be part of this society?

- How does Lord Illingworth illustrate the responsibilities of a rich and powerful man? (You might remember here that he has, for reasons of his own, offered to marry Mrs Arbuthnot, and to leave his properties to Gerald.)

- What sort of behaviour do you think he might get away with, judging by Lady Hunstanton's comments?

Can you see a combination here of power, and of age and birthright, and of being male in this sexist society?

Wilde adds a little more detail to show the power of this sort of society. The politician, Mr Kelvil shares their company, although he says in Act 1 that whilst he thinks Lord Illingworth is a 'very brilliant man', he thinks he is 'lacking' in 'purity of life'. Nevertheless, although his concern for social issues is mocked by Illingworth, Mr Kelvil is happy to be part of their company. Also present is Dr Daubeny, the Archdeacon, who says in Act 2 'I have never enjoyed myself more.'

ACTIVITY 18

What do you think that the presence of these men implies about the status of this society? You might think about:

- whether there is a suggestion that both the politicians and the Church are happy with the social structure, and with attitudes within this structure

- whether their presence might imply criticism of the Church and of politicians for supporting the existing social structure.

To develop this context further you might think about the discussion in Act 2 between the ladies about the 'ideal man', and also work out how Wilde presents Lord Illingworth as such an attractive character, through the Lord's wit and laid-back attitude to life. You might also think about how self-satisfied this society is; you can see this when characters who do not fit in, the Arbuthnots and Hester Worsley, are banished at the end of the play.

The psychological/moral context

In this context, which may be attractive to a modern reader, Wilde may be seen to offer radical criticism of this society. This aspect is developed through the characters of Mrs Arbuthnot, Gerald and Hester Worsley. In this reading, the play fractures, and the easy social comedy is stopped in Act 3, when Lord Illingworth and Mrs Arbuthnot confront each other, and in the serious tone of Act 4.

Mrs Arbuthnot has suffered greatly for her social sins of an affair with the young Lord Illingworth, and the birth of her illegitimate child. You will see in this play that this society makes women pay. Mrs Arbuthnot has several long, melodramatic speeches which stop the onward movement of the play. At the end of Act 3 she exclaims how she is a 'lost soul'. Then she explains her life to Gerald using biblical images, for example:

It may be that I am too bound to him already, [Lord Illingworth] who, robbing me, yet left me richer, so that in the mire of my life, I found the pearl of price, or what I thought would be so.

The reference to the 'pearl' is drawn from the Bible, and you need to work through the lady's long speeches to work out all the biblical images such as those to Hannah and Samuel, and to being cast out naked. The reference to the pearl is interesting because the other 'good' female in the play is Hester Worsley. An educated member of the audience might know that Hester was a lady in a similar situation to Mrs Arbuthnot in a novel called *The Scarlet Letter* by Nathaniel Hawthorne. This novel was published in 1850 to great acclaim, and Hawthorne became part of English society when he became US Consul to

England in 1853. He would have become one of the important and established writers for students such as Oscar Wilde and for educated members of society to read. In *The Scarlet Letter* Hester's child was called Pearl, and Hawthorne showed Hester's saintly qualities in contrast to the horrid society she lived in. Perhaps some of the audience, and also modern readers, would realise this link, and would take these two female characters seriously, in contrast to the entertaining females in the play, as examples of sound morality. In addition, Lady Hunstanton says in Act 4 that Mrs Arbuthnot 'has the room of a sweet saint'.

ACTIVITY 19

What do you make of Lady Hunstanton's attitude and that of Lord Illingworth to Mrs Arbuthnot? What might be implied by her 'expulsion' from this society and their intended flight to America?

It might be interesting to think about the title of the play here: *A Woman of No Importance*. Throughout the play there are changing references to the title. As you have seen, she has great dramatic importance; in Act 3 she is very important to Gerald as she influences his decision by revealing his parenthood. And at the end of the play Lord Illingworth pleads to her to bring his son and himself together: 'You can do it if you choose.'

ACTIVITY 20

Think about the balance of power between these two characters and consider:

- What is the situation of Lord Illingworth here?

- Can you see any irony in the difference between Lord Illingworth's power in society, and within his blood ties?

The clearest statement of the power reversal occurs when Mrs Arbuthnot repeats Lord Illingworth's words of warning about children which he spoke to her in Act 2, when he thought he had won over his son. She repeats these lines at the end of the play:

'Don't be deceived, George. Children begin by loving their parents. After a time they judge them. Rarely if ever do they forgive them.'

Clearly she has won here, and can truly say that the Lord is 'A man of no importance'. The stage directions stress how dazed he is by his 'punishment', a term of moral justice. Are you able to see how the word 'importance' effectively creates an opposition between Lord Illingworth's power socially and, effectively, morally? On this level, the play has become a morality tale, and you could carry on here by exploring the character and role of Hester Worsley.

The dramatic context of the play as comedy

Usually, in a traditional comedy, such as Shakespeare's *Twelfth Night,* there are three distinct stages in the development of the play and of society. These are the first stage of a disordered society or a society with something wrong about it; then a stage of confusion and doubt; then a final stage of reconciliation and harmony, when difficulties and injustices are sorted out.

ACTIVITY 21

Think about how this idea applies to Wilde's play:

- Is there disorder at first, when Lord Illingworth doesn't know he has a son? Is the society fair when women get such a raw deal?

- Is there confusion as Lord Illingworth, Gerald and Mrs Arbuthnot learn the complicated truth of things?

- Is there any sense of social justice finally, or do things carry on as before?

- Is there any sense that the society has improved morally? Is there a reshaping to include elements of duty, honesty and family love?

This concludes the study of *contexts* for this play. However there are others including the *dramatic context of structure*. Here you might carry out an analysis of how the play proceeds with balanced episodes (e.g. the discussion of the ideal man in Act 2, and the ideal woman in Act 3); with the use of repetition as we have seen; the shifting balance between melodrama and comedy; the tension caused by conflict with some very tense moments.

There is the *social context of parenting* which arises in the contrasts between Mrs Arbuthnot's self-sacrificing view of parenting, and Lord Illingworth's commercial view of this. Finally, there is the *social context of male–male relationships*, and the homo-erotic element of Lord Illingworth's attraction towards Gerald, and the young man's response to this. These are some of the several contexts which may relate to this play, and you may well continue to discover more. There is, finally, a last distinction to be made, seen in Lady Hunstanton's words to Gerald in Act 4:

'You would see the world – as much of it, at least, as one should look at …'

This could be Oscar Wilde's warning to his audience: you may see the play, but to understand it, you have to look at it very carefully indeed. This is perhaps exactly what the upper-class members of this self-satisfied society fail to do as they continue in their rather uncaring way.

Summary

This section has included several different sorts of contexts in drama. You will have realised that those chosen for exploration in this module are examples which you will need to develop further. Also there are other contexts, and many other readings to be found within the plays. You could use the models presented in this module to guide you through the play you are studying.

Post 1900 Drama

As explained in the introduction to this module, four Assessment Objectives are tested in this part of the examination paper. You will have to 'communicate clearly the knowledge, understanding and insight appropriate to literary study, using appropriate terminology and accurate and coherent written expression' (AO1), 'respond with knowledge and understanding' (AO2i), 'show detailed understanding of the ways in which writers' choices of form, structure and language shape meanings' (AO3), and 'articulate independent opinions and judgements informed by different interpretations of literary texts by other readers' (AO4). This section carries 20% of the marks for the AS course. The dominant Assessment Objective in this section is AO4, which carries 10 of the 20 percentage points available, with the other 10 points split between the other three Objectives. A key consideration is AO3, however, as an understanding of the writers' skills and meanings will form the material for demonstrating AOs 2i and 3, and the basis for arriving at 'independent opinions and judgements'. This section, therefore, will deal with these features first, before going on to consider how you can meet AO4 in the examination.

Form

A narrator can be used by the writer to tell parts of the story, to fill in background, to indicate time changes, to comment on events and characters and to draw lessons for the audience, in other words, to 'frame' the action in a number of ways.

In *The Glass Menagerie*, Tennessee Williams uses the narrator, Tom, to do all of these things, and to act as a character in the drama himself. Here are some of his comments from his opening speech:

> To begin with, I turn back time. I reverse it to that quaint period, the thirties, when the huge middle class of America was matriculating in a school for the blind.

As well as signalling the play's time-shift, Williams uses the narrator to give a socio-historical background, and the playwright's attitude to it. A further remark in the speech is: 'This is the social background of the play.'

Here, something of the nature and the mood of the play, and the dramatic presentation, are sketched in for the audience:

> The play is memory.
> Being a memory play, it is dimly lighted, it is sentimental, it is not realistic.

In this introductory speech the narrator is used to comment on the characters, including himself. There are also signals to the audience about the family's world of illusion, on the importance to the action of the character who doesn't appear, and on the symbolic significance of the gentleman caller; in this last function, the narrator is also speaking for the writer, perhaps.

> I am the narrator of the play, and also a character in it.
>
> [*The gentleman caller*] … is the most realistic character in the play, being an emissary from a world of reality that we were somehow set apart from … since I have a poet's weakness for symbols, I am using this character also as a symbol.
>
> There is a fifth character in the play who doesn't appear …
>
> This is our father.

Read the following extract from Scene 5 of *The Glass Menagerie* and then work through Activity 22.

> TOM [*to the audience*] Across the alley from us was the Paradise Dance Hall. On evenings in spring the windows and doors were open and the music came outdoors. Sometimes the lights were turned out except for a large glass sphere that hung from the ceiling. It would turn slowly about and filter the dusk with delicate rainbow colours. Then the orchestra played a waltz or a tango, something that had a slow and sensuous rhythm. Couples would come outside, to the relative privacy of the alley. You could see them kissing behind ash-pits and telegraph poles.
>
> This was the compensation for lives that passed like mine, without any change or adventure.
>
> Adventure and change were imminent in this year. They were waiting around the corner for all these kids.
>
> Suspended in the mist over Berchtesgaden, caught in the folds of Chamberlain's umbrella –
>
> In Spain there was Guernica!
>
> But here there was only hot swing music and liquor, dance halls, bars, and movies, and sex that hung in the gloom like a chandelier and flooded the world with brief, deceptive rainbows …
>
> All the world was waiting for bombardments!

ACTIVITY 22

Now try to analyse this passage and make notes on:

1 information given to the audience about place

2 creation of mood, as a background to the action

3 the narrator's own situation

4 information about the socio-historical context

5 how expectancy and tension are created in the audience.

Setting is a key element of dramatic form. Unlike poetry and prose, drama is visual, and setting, conveyed through stage directions, is what the audience sees first. It can therefore be used to shape meanings. In Brian Friel's *Making History*, for example, the opening description of the set is:

A large living room in O'NEILL'S *home in Dungannon, County Tyrone, Ireland. Late August in 1591. The room is spacious and scantily furnished: a large, refectory-type table; some chairs and stools; a sideboard. No attempt at decoration.*

O'NEILL *moves around this comfortless room quickly and energetically, inexpertly cutting the stems off flowers, thrusting the flowers into various vases and then adding water. He is not listening to* HARRY HOVEDEN *who consults and reads from various papers on the table.*

At the beginning of Scene 2, however, the same set has changed considerably:

Almost a year has passed. The same room as in Scene 1, but MABEL *has added to the furnishings and the room is now more comfortable and more colourful.*

MABEL *is sitting alone doing delicate and complicated lacework. She works in silence for some time. Then from offstage the sudden and terrifying sound of a young girl shrieking. This is followed immediately by boisterous laughter, shouting, horseplay and a rapid exchange in Irish between a young girl and a young man.*

'Added', 'comfortable', and 'colourful', the opposites of 'scantily' and comfortless', all suggest the effect on Hugh's life of the arrival of Mabel. This is not all, however. The audience will clearly see this change – after all, the action is in the same place – but the atmosphere has changed, too. In the opening, Hugh 'inexpertly' cuts the flowers; Mabel's 'delicate and complicated' work indicates artistic accomplishment. Hugh and Harry are concerned with papers; Mabel's activity is artistic, though, and the sounds of the 'young girl', coupled with 'boisterous laughter, shouting, horseplay', suggest a very different scene.

The change from the end of Act 1 to Act 2 Scene 1 forms an even sharper contrast:

[O'DONNELL *dashes on.*]

O'DONNELL   A messenger from Spain outside, Hugh! [*To* MABEL] It gets better by the minute! [*To* O'NEILL] The Spanish fleet sails on September 3! [*To* MABEL] Maybe you speak Spanish? You should hear your man out there: 'Beeg fleet – beeg ships'!

O'NEILL   Where do they sail from?

O'DONNELL   Lisbon. On the first tide.

O'NEILL   And where do they land?

[HARRY *enters.*]

HARRY   Did you call me?

O'NEILL   Where do they land?

O'DONNELL   'Keen-sall.'

O'NEILL   Where – where?

O'DONNELL   'Keen-sall' – Kinsale, I suppose.

O'NEILL   Oh, God, no.

O'DONNELL   Wherever Kinsale is. This is it, Mabel darling! This is it! Yipeeeeee!

[*Quick black.*]

ACT 2 Scene 1

About eight months later. The edge of a thicket somewhere near the Sperrin mountains.

O'NEILL *is on his knees. He is using a wooden box as a table and he is writing – scoring out – writing rapidly, with total concentration, almost frantically. Various loose pages on the ground beside him. He looks tired and anxious and harassed. He is so concentrated on his writing that he is unaware of* O'DONNELL'S *entrance. Then, when he is aware, he reaches perfunctorily for the dagger at his side.*

O'DONNELL, *too, looks tired and anxious. He is also spattered with mud and his boots are sodden.*

O'DONNELL   It's only me. I suppose you thought something had happened to me.

O'NEILL   You were longer than you thought.

O'DONNELL I had to make detours going and coming back – the countryside's crawling with troops. And then there were a lot of things to see to at home – disputes – documents – the usual. Look at my feet. These Sperrins aren't mountains – they're bloody bogs! I suppose you wouldn't have a spare pair of boots?

ACTIVITY 23

1 How are speed and excitement conveyed in the language and action of the end of Act 1? Why do you think the light change is instructed to be 'quick black'?

2 Which words in the stage directions for the beginning of Act 2 suggest a very different atmosphere?

3 What does O'Neill's reaction to O'Donnell's appearance indicate?

4 How is the language at the beginning of Act 2 different from the language at the end of Act 1?

Stage directions, and the ways they are followed by actors and directors, can be used to establish or change mood. Here are the stage directions at the end of Act 2 of *Comedians*:

[*Chants.*] Lou Macari, Lou Macari … I shoulda smashed him. They allus mek you feel sorry for 'em, out in the open. I suppose I shoulda just kicked him without looking at him. [*Pause. He looks after them. Calling.*] National Unity? Up yours, sunshine. [*Pause. He picks up a tiny violin, i.e. another, switched, uncrushed, and a bow. Addresses it. Plays 'The Red Flag' – very simple and direct.*] Still, I made the buggers laugh. …

[PRICE *walks off. The* CONCERT SECRETARY, *probably shocked, embarrassed, not wishing to dwell. Lights fade.* WATERS *stands, face gaunt, grey.* CHALLENOR *tosses down a scotch, sheafs his notes, pockets pen.*]

CONCERT SECRETARY That's the lot, ladies and gentlemen. You have your cards, I think. Charlie Shaw has 'em for them that hasn't, and we're starting right away, settle yourselves down, now. And it's eyes down for a full house. … [*Lights fade gradually.*] Always look after … Number One. [*Lights fade to black.*]

The comedy of Gethin's act has been replaced by hatred. The stage directions indicate different voices – chanting, calling, speaking. Both the audience and the now invisible dummies are addressed. The violin is a surprise – the audience have assumed it to be broken. All this, together with 'I made the buggers laugh' mean the audience are not likely to laugh at all, and this is reinforced by the directed responses of the three watchers – 'shocked, embarrassed, not wishing to dwell'. This clearly informs how the audience might react. The Secretary's language is different, and belongs to a different type of performance, though the writer carefully makes it relevant to what has preceded it: 'Always look after … Number One' is a version of 'National Unity? Up yours, sunshine'. The gradual fade suggests that the scene continues.

Here are the opening directions of Act 3 of *Comedians*:

Classroom. Time: 9.43. Empty.

McBrain, Samuels *and* Connor *return slowly, to sit in their respective places, though an almost deliberate distance apart.* Phil Murray *in. They sit, glum, drained, separate.*

Simple exhaustion underpins the low, tense, anxious, angry, baffled mood of the four. No eye contacts. People sit or fiddle. Samuels *sits in his coat, ready for away.* Connor *is again pretty wet.* McBrain *has changed back to his parka and jeans, his bag on the desk in front of him.*

Price, *off, suddenly starts up with 'There's no business like show business …'*

ACTIVITY 24

1 Why do you think this scene begins with an empty room?

2 Which words tell you about the moods of McBrain, Samuels and Connor? Think about actions as well as emotional words.

3 What effect do you think the offstage song might have – both on the characters and the audience?

Tennessee Williams uses a screen on to which are projected images or legends, to shape meanings for the audience. Here is an example from Scene 1:

Amanda   … Among my callers were some of the most prominent young planters of the Mississippi delta – planters and sons of planters!

[Tom *motions for music and a spot of light on* Amanda. *Her eyes lift, her face glows, her voice becomes rich and elegiac.*

screen legend: 'Où sont les neiges'.]

The narrator is used here as a director of stage effects. The screen legend (a quotation from a nostalgic fifteenth-century French ballad by Villon) shows that Amanda's mind is deep in a memory of the past, but the mood of nostalgia evoked by the words of the poem, together with the stage directions to the actress playing Amanda, also invite a view of the character as lost in the past, feeling a deep sense of loss.

ACTIVITY 25

TOM: I like a lot of adventure.

[IMAGE ON SCREEN: SAILING VESSEL WITH JOLLY ROGER.]

AMANDA: Most young men find adventure in their careers.

Reading this short piece of dialogue, what does the sailing vessel suggest to you about Tom's desires? Why the *Jolly Roger*?

Contrast this with Tom's current existence, and think about the effect of Amanda's remark on the audience's view of the image, and of Tom.

Another device Williams uses is the transparent fourth wall, which ascends during the opening scene and descends again during the closing scene. Through this the audience observes the action, and the closed, isolated world in which Amanda and Laura live is emphasised. The possibility of release has been removed by the end of the play, as the wall descends once again.

Music is used extensively by Tennessee Williams in *The Glass Menagerie*, largely, as he says in the Production Notes, 'to give emotional emphasis to suitable passages'. In Scene 5, for example, the stage direction '*The Dance-Hall music changes to a tango that has a minor and somewhat ominous tone*' clearly indicates the way music is being used. As a dramatist, Williams also makes careful use of sound effects.

This passage from Scene 6 of *The Glass Menagerie* shows a number of stage effects working together. The shy, withdrawn Laura is being called in to meet a 'gentleman caller' whom she knows, and doesn't want to face.

AMANDA: You're keeping us waiting, honey! We can't say grace until you come to the table!

The back door is pushed weakly open and LAURA *comes in. She is obviously quite faint, her lips trembling, her eyes wide and staring. She moves unsteadily toward the table.*

LEGEND: 'TERROR!'

Outside a summer storm is coming abruptly. The white curtains billow inward at the windows and there is a sorrowful murmur and deep blue dusk.

> LAURA *suddenly stumbles – she catches at a chair with a faint moan.*
>
> TOM: Laura!
>
> AMANDA: Laura!
>
> *There is a clap of thunder.*
>
> LEGEND: 'AH!'

ACTIVITY 26

Examine the ways in which the various elements in this passage – the legends, the storm, the movement of the curtains, the sound effect of the murmur, the colours, and the thunder – create the atmosphere which underscores the emotions of the characters on stage.

Voice is also important in drama in shaping meaning. In *Making History*, the stage directions are very specific about O'Donnell's reading of O'Neill's submission, mentioned above:

> *At first* O'DONNELL *reads his portion of the submission in mocking and exaggerated tones. He is unaware that* O'NEILL *is deadly serious. But as they proceed through the document –* O'DONNELL *reading his sections,* O'NEILL *speaking his by heart –* O'DONNELL'S *good humour drains away and he ends up as formal and as grave as* O'NEILL.

O'Donnell's gradual change of tone shows his gradual realisation of the seriousness of the submission – the audience will notice this too, and the change in O'Donnell. Friel uses voice in a similar way at the end of the play, when O'Neill repeats his submission:

> *When* O'NEILL *speaks he speaks almost in a whisper in counterpoint to* LOMBARD'S *public recitation. His English accent gradually fades until at the end his accent is pure Tyrone.*

The change in O'Neill's accent may be interpreted as an acknowledgement of his roots – and his betrayal of them.

Drama, unlike poetry and prose, often conveys meaning without words. The purest form of this is mime, used several times in Trevor Griffiths' play *Comedians*.

The door opens and the CARETAKER *peeps in, sees the room vacated, advances. He carries a smashed chair, the frame in the right hand, a leg in the left.*

After a moment he sights PATEL'S *muslin-covered package. Stops, scans. Signs of slight but rising apprehension. He reaches gingerly towards it with the chair leg. Touches. Prods more vigorously, yet still cringing from it, as though half-expecting an explosion. Nothing. He drops the chair leg, opens the neck of the bag, peers in, sniffs, sniffs again, sniffs several times, his face crinkling with disgust. Stands. Picks up his chair. Leaves, switching off all lights behind him.*

The stage directions here show that the actions tell an emotional story – a comic one, of course. The stop and scan shows 'apprehension'. 'Gingerly' and 'cringing' characterise his 'half-expecting' touch. The action of 'sniffing' (repeated for effect) conveys his 'disgust'. The silent exit with the bits of the chair forms a comic closure to the Act.

Here is part of Gethin Price's act in Act 2:

He brings the bow finally to his mouth, tries to bite the thread off, his teeth are set on edge, he winces mutely, tries again, can't. He thinks. Tries, bending oddly on one leg, to trap the thread under his huge boot. Fails. Thinks. Takes out a lighter. Sets fire to the thread. Satisfaction. Makes as if to play. The cocked bow slowly begins to smoulder at the far end. He waves it about, horrified. The violin now begins to play unaided in his other hand a piece of intricate Bach. He's trapped for a moment between the two events; finally he places the spent bow on the stage, puts the violin under his boot, dimps it like a cigarette until it's thoroughly crushed.

ACTIVITY 27

Work out how the actions convey the emotions in this piece of mime.

Action is often used to convey emotion. In *Making History* O'Donnell is reading O'Neill's submission to the Queen:

O'DONNELL   [*Reads*] To whom I now most abjectly and most obediently offer my services and indeed … my life … [*Silence. Then* O'NEILL *moves away as if to distance himself from what he has just said.*]

O'Neill thinks of what he has done as betrayal; he moves physically away from the proof of it.

In *Comedians*, a prop, in this case a shattered lectern, is used to make a gag:

> [*The* CARETAKER *comes in. He carries a shattered lectern.*]
>
> CARETAKER [*to* WATERS] I told the Principal you were looking for him. [*He points in* PATEL'S *direction.*] He's back now. He had to go down to the other centre in Beswick. [*He makes a drinking sign with his right hand.*]
>
> WATERS Thank you, I think we can manage now …
>
> CARETAKER I told him you were looking. He's in his office. Waiting.
>
> WATERS It's very good of you.
>
> CARETAKER [*looking at lectern*] They've gone bloody *mad* down there, that Karate lot. [*He leaves.*]

Like all humour, the success lies in the technique – the Caretaker doesn't mention the shattered lectern until he's about to leave. The technique here is the writer's, not the Caretaker's.

Structure

'Structure' refers to the variety of techniques the dramatist has used in constructing the play, which help to shape meanings for the audience. Finding structures in a play (or a poem or a novel) is best achieved by thinking about patterns, for example, where similar scenes or combinations of characters or dialogue recur, and perhaps change.

The simplest overall structure in the plays being considered here is probably Trevor Griffiths' *Comedians*. The action takes place on the same evening, at three different times – before, during and after the club performances. This also dictates the nature of the action: preparing for the show, the show itself (in a different place), and the characters' reflection on it. The comedy performances are the centre of it – and it is the nature of comedy which is the centre of the play.

Making History has a more wide-ranging structure, in terms of time and place. Only the first two scenes take place in the same setting, and here the difference over time is marked – see page 118 above. The third scene is in a very different place, and mood (see Activity 23 above). The final scene is many years later, in a different country, and with a very changed central figure, evident from the first moment of the scene. The stages of Hugh's life, and the changes, are at the heart of the play – what will history show of them, and what should it show?

The central structural device in *The Glass Menagerie* is the narrator, who links the scenes, and even when he doesn't, the scenes flow from one to the next in an uninterrupted chronological sequence in the same place, though different areas within the place are used at different times. The use of the 'fourth wall', which was mentioned on page 122, has a structural significance. Because the audience has seen the wall being removed at the beginning, when it descends in the last scene a sense of closure is produced. This is doubly significant as Amanda and Laura have both been offered a possibility of escape during the action, only to be closed in again by the end.

In *The Glass Menagerie* Tennessee Williams uses Tom, the narrator, to explore the theme of time. In his opening speech he says: 'To begin with, I turn back time. I reverse it to that quaint period, the thirties, when the huge middle class of time was matriculating in a school for the blind'. Tom signals his structural role here and also, in the second sentence, there is an indication of how it will happen, when he switches from present tense, 'I reverse' to past tense, 'was matriculating'.

ACTIVITY 28

The Glass Menagerie is a 'memory play', as Tom informs the audience in the first scene. At the end, the play emerges from memories:

TOM … It always came upon me unawares, taking me altogether by surprise. Perhaps it was a familiar bit of music. Perhaps it was only a piece of transparent glass –

Perhaps I am walking along a street at night …

1 Why might the music or the glass evoke memories, and take Tom into the past again?

2 How is the switch back from past time to present time shown?

Similarly, the subject of the nature of history in *Making History* is raised very early in the play, but is presented sharply again at the end:

LOMBARD I'm no historian, Hugh. I'm not even sure I know what the historian's function is – not to talk of his method.

O'NEILL But you'll tell the truth?

LOMBARD If you're asking me will my story be as accurate as possible – of course it will. But are truth and falsity the proper criteria? I don't know. Maybe when the time comes my first responsibility will be to tell the best possible narrative. Isn't that what history is, a kind of story-telling?

O'NEILL Is it?

| LOMBARD | Imposing a pattern on events that were mostly casual and haphazard and shaping them into a narrative that is logical and interesting. Oh, yes, I think so. |
| O'NEILL | And where does the truth come into all this? |

Questions are raised here – what is the function of history? How does the historian work? What does the reader of history require? And should history be the truth, whatever that means? These ideas are returned to throughout the play, until Hugh reads the opening of Lombard's history of his own life at the end of the play. The answers to his questioning – at least in this play – are rendered in dramatic form.

Here is the opening and the ending of Act 2 Scene 2 of *Making History*:

O'NEILL *is now in his early sixties. His eyesight is beginning to trouble him – he carries a walking stick. And he drinks too much. We first hear his raucous shouting off. When he enters we see that he is slightly drunk. His temper is volatile and bitter and dangerous. He is carrying a lighted taper.*

and

O'NEILL	May it please you to mitigate your just indignation against me for my betrayal of you which deserves no forgiveness and for which I can make no satisfaction, even with my life –
LOMBARD	And people reflected in their minds that when he would reach manhood there would not be one like him of the Irish to avenge their wrongs and punish the plunderings of his race –
O'NEILL	Mabel, I am sorry … please forgive me, Mabel …
LOMBARD	For it was foretold by prophets and by predictors of futurity that there would come one like him –
	A man, glorious, pure, faithful above all Who will cause mournful weeping in every territory. He will be a God-like prince And he will be king for the span of his life.
	[O'NEILL *is now crying. Bring down the lights slowly.*]

ACTIVITY 29

1 Look at the words that Lombard uses in his history to describe O'Neill. How does the description of O'Neill at the beginning of the scene suggest that the words do not match the reality?

2 What is there in O'Neill's words and actions at the end which do not match Lombard's description?

3 There are several structural choices made by the writer here. Why do you think he has chosen to begin the scene with O'Neill alone and drunk, and to end it like this? Why do you think the playwright chooses to show O'Neill with a lighted taper at the beginning, and to make the final stage direction 'Bring down the lights slowly'? Why does he choose to end the play on this moment?

The placing of the expression of central ideas in the play is clearly a structural decision which helps to shape meaning. In Act 1 of *Comedians*, several of the comedians make jokes which are 'against' members of society – women, homosexuals, etc. Waters, in showing them that such jokes are wrong because they are based 'upon a distortion', exposes the truth behind the jokes:

WATERS [*finally, mild, matter-of-fact*] I've never liked the Irish, you know. Dr. Johnson said they were a very truthful race, they never spoke well of each other, but then how could they have? [*They look around, faintly puzzled, amused.*] Big, thick, stupid heads, large cabbage ears, hairy nostrils, daft eyes, fat, flapping hands, stinking of soil and Guinness. The niggers of Europe. Huge, uncontrollable wangers, spawning their degenerate kind wherever they're allowed to settle. I'd stop them settling here if I had my way. Send 'em back to the primordial bog they came from. Potato heads.

[*Pause.* McBRAIN *clenches and unclenches his fists on the desk, watches them carefully.*]

Having placed this (and two other examples) in the mind of the audience, the playwright can rely on this to inform their response to the jokes the comedians resort to when playing to the club audience:

SAMUELLS … Heard about the Irish lamp post? Pissed on a dog. Hear about the Irish cargo ship carrying yoyos? Sank forty-four times. The Irish waterpolo team. Drowned twelve horses. This secretary runs into the boss's office and says, Can I use your dictaphone? He says, No, use your finger like everyone else! There's this West Indian tries to get a labouring job on a building site. Foreman says, No chance, I know you lot. I give one of you a job, you turn up the next day with a gang of your friends. He begs and pleads and finally he gets the job. Next day he turns up with a pigmy. [*Indicating.*] Pigmy. Down there. The foreman said, What did I tell you, no friends! He says, That's not my friend, that's my lunch. What do you think of this Women's Lib, then? Burnt your bras have you? Did you, sir, how interesting. I burnt the wife's. She went bloody mad, she was still in it.

ACTIVITY 30

Who are the jokes 'against' here, and how? What exactly is being suggested about the people in the jokes?

Language

One of the functions of language in drama is to convey character. The following passage from Act 1 Scene 1 of *Making History*, for example, establishes the character of O'Donnell early in the play:

HARRY	You sit there, Hugh.
O'DONNELL	Damn it, maybe I could poison him! The very job! Send him a peace offering – a cask of Bordeaux special!
LOMBARD	Has everybody got a copy?
O'DONNELL	Or better still you [O'NEILL] send him the Bordeaux. He'd never suspect you. I got a jar of this deadly stuff from Genoa last week – just one drop in your glass and – plunk!
HARRY	Go ahead, Peter.
LOMBARD	Thank you. Three months –
O'DONNELL	All the same that jacket takes years off him.
LOMBARD	If I may, Hugh [O'DONNELL] –
O'DONNELL	You would never think he was forty-one, would you? Almost forty-two. [*Offering* LOMBARD *the floor*] Peter.
LOMBARD	Three months ago you [O'NEILL] wrote again to Philip asking for Spanish arms and money. You have a copy – dated May 14 last.
O'DONNELL	I have no copy.
	[HARRY *points to a paper in front of* O'DONNELL.]
	Ah. Sorry.

The three exclamation marks in O'Donnell's first speech here typify O'Donnell's excitable nature, as does the exaggeration ('just one drop in your glass and – plunk!') and the strong emotions in his first two speeches. His mind is volatile, shifting quickly from one thing to another – 'all the same that jacket takes years off him'. He is not particularly observant, and possibly quick to take offence – 'I have no copy', but equally quick to forgive, as 'Ah. Sorry' shows.

As in poetry or prose, figurative language is used by writers to make the audience reflect on meanings. Tennessee Williams, for example, uses symbolism extensively in *The Glass Menagerie*. In his opening speech the narrator says he has 'a poet's weakness for symbols', and that the gentleman caller should be seen as a symbol. The importance of the glass menagerie as a symbol for Laura and her life is signalled by its use in the title, and Laura mentions that she has been spending most of her time in 'that big glass-house' – a phrase the audience might well be reminded of when the transparent fourth wall descends at the end of the play. She is described as she is preparing for Jim's visit as being '*like a piece of translucent glass touched by light, given a momentary radiance, not actual, not lasting*'. The hope that Jim brings will not last, either. When the glass unicorn's horn is broken, Laura says 'Now it is just like all the other horses', and that it will feel 'less – freakish!' Clearly the glass animal is a symbol of Laura herself here.

In Scene 4 of *The Glass Menagerie*, Tom describes the magician's stage act:

> TOM   … But the wonderfullest trick of all was the coffin trick. We nailed him into a coffin and he got out of the coffin without removing one nail. [*He has come inside.*] There is a trick that would come in handy for me – get out of this 2 by 4 situation! … You know it don't take much intelligence to get yourself into a nailed-up coffin, Laura. But who in hell ever got himself out of one without removing one nail?
>
> [*As if in answer, the father's grinning photograph lights up.*]

ACTIVITY 31

1 When does Tom first liken his situation to being in a coffin?

2 How are the family 'nailed-up' by their situation?

3 How did the father get out of the 'coffin'?

4 If the coffin symbolises the family's situation, and their apartment, how might the audience interpret the descent of the wall at the end of the play? Remember throughout all this the obvious connotations of the word 'coffin'.

Seeds are used as metaphors for people, in a way, in *Making History*. When they are first mentioned, qualities are attributed to them, but apparently just in the 'natural' sense:

> MARY   Don't plant the fennel near the dill or the two will cross-fertilize.
>
> MABEL   Is that bad?
>
> MARY   You'll end up with a seed that's neither one thing or the other. Borage likes the sun but it will survive wherever you plant it – it's very tough.

Further on in the play the qualities of the seeds are used to reflect on characters:

> HARRY   You want it known that you've promised Maguire you'd help him?
>
> O'NEILL   I don't think I told her that, did I? [*Reads*:] 'The coriander seed. Watch this seed carefully as it ripens suddenly and will fall without warning.' Sounds like Maguire, doesn't it? – Coriander Maguire.
>
> HARRY   Because if you renege on that promise he certainly will fall.
>
> O'NEILL   What herb are you, Harry? What about dill? 'Has a comforting and soothing effect.' Close enough. And who is borage? 'Inclined to induce excessive courage, even recklessness.' That's O'Donnell, isn't it? Borage O'Donnell.

ACTIVITY 32

This connection has two effects.

1 This is a play with the same characters in three time periods. How is the idea of seeds useful in such a play?

2 The seeds' descriptions help to define the characters for the audience. If you're studying the play, consider how the seed descriptions of dill and borage apply to Harry and O'Donnell.

Word play is a source of humour, helping to shape tone. There are different types of word play – plays made with the sound of words, or the ideas of words, or the associations of words. Overleaf are several examples of word play in *Comedians*.

1

McBRAIN	Nobody'll fail me. I'm unfailable.
CONNOR	Hark at the Pope, now.

2

McBRAIN	Crème de la crème.
SAMUELS	A little clotted here and there perhaps.

3

PHIL	What you watching *Crossroads* for?
GED	It helps me sleep.

4

WATERS	. . . Willy.
PHIL	Willy Nilly.
GED	Willy Won'ty.
PRICE	Willy Nocomebackagain.
CONNOR	Willy Ell.
SAMUELS	[*pulling face*] God Villy ...
McBRAIN	[*same face*] Willy Nands.

ACTIVITY 33

Look at each of these word plays carefully. Are they based on the sound of words, or associations of words, or the ideas that the words suggest?

The language forms of comedy are used in *Comedians*. When McBrain arrives in the classroom, his first words are 'De Da!'. The comedians fall easily into the language forms of jokes, as in this exchange:

CONNOR	What's wrong with the suit? It's a bit wet …
SAMUELS	S'hard to put your finger on …
McBRAIN	… as the actress said to the bishop …
	[*Groan.*]

The actress and the bishop are stock characters in this sort of sexual innuendo. Humour can also depend on words building up expectations, then knocking them down, as in the following passage.

Here is an excerpt from McBrain's act in the club:

There's this very brilliant Irishman. From Dublin. I tried to get the wife to come. It gets harder, I dunnit though. I don't say she's jealous but she's the only woman I know. If music be the food of love, how about a bite of your maracas? I was in bed with the wife last Thursday. The wife lay there, very quiet, smoking her pipe. I leaned across and I said, Do you fancy anything, heart? And she said, Yes, I fancy an African about six-foot-three with a big fat … cheque book. [*To audience.*] Don't get ahead of yourselves!

ACTIVITY 34

Find all the ways in which the audience's expectations might be played with here. For each example you find, decide what the audience might have expected, and what might have led them to this – the words or the situation.

When Waters exposes the attitudes that lie behind jokes, the language changes completely. In the passage in the activity above, the language is comfortable, colloquial and belongs to speech: 'I leaned across and I said, Do you fancy anything, heart?'. Waters deliberately uses language which is unfunny, uncomfortable, and hostile:

Negroes. Cripples. Defectives. The mad. Women. [*Turning deliberately to* MURRAY'S *row.*] Workers. Dirty. Unschooled. Shifty. Grabbing all they can get. Putting coal in the bath. Chips with everything. Chips and beer. Trade Unions dedicated to maximizing wages and minimizing work. Strikes for the idle. Their greed. And their bottomless stupidity.

> **AO4: articulate independent opinions and judgements informed by different interpretations of literary texts by other readers**

This is the most important Assessment Objective for the twentieth-century texts on this paper, carrying 10 of the 20 marks available. Questions are likely to give a view of the text and the writer, and ask for your opinion. A question might well direct you to one particular scene to think about. Before considering how you might plan your answer, it's worth thinking about the kinds of subjects that might crop up. Broadly, they could focus on the writer's concerns, and how the writer presents them; the writer's techniques; or the qualities of the writer's work. Here is a list of some of the things which could form the focus of questions about Tennessee Williams, Trevor Griffiths and Brian Friel. This is not an exhaustive list, by any means.

The Glass Menagerie

- illusions
- the American Dream
- the grip of the past
- Williams's use of stage directions and effect
- Williams's use of symbolism.

Comedians

- the nature and uses of comedy
- the importance of truth
- attitudes in society to other genders/races/attitudes
- the relationship between stage and audience
- how Griffiths uses structure and language in the play.

Making History

- what historical truth means
- how history is written, and why
- the purposes of history
- nationalism
- idealism v. pragmatism
- how Friel uses structure in the play
- how Friel uses setting in the play.

Forming a response

As an example, let's suppose that you were studying *Comedians*, and that the question you were going to tackle was:

'Although the play is called Comedians, *and is about comedy, it is not comic at all; on the contrary, Griffiths has created a disturbing, depressing piece of theatre. It is horrid.'* To what extent do you agree with this view of the play?

You know that:

• you have to consider this view of the play

• you have to write about form, structure and language, not just the effect of the play the word 'created' indicates this

• you must come to an 'independent opinion' about how far the play is 'disturbing, depressing' and 'horrid', and how far it is 'comic'.

There are a number of ways to structure your response, but you would need to think about some of these elements:

• how Griffiths creates disturbing theatre – you might consider the nature and effect of Gethin's act, and the effect of it being placed in the centre of the play; the details of the act, such as the piercing of the dolls and the bleeding; and Waters's experiences in the concentration camp

• how the play might be thought of as depressing – you might consider the effects of the settings; the nature of the jokes that are approved of by Challenor; the aggressive stereotypes that the comics resort to under pressure

• the elements of the play that could be thought of as 'horrid' – you might consider the ways that Waters exposes the truth behind jokes in Act 1; the ways that the comics are shown to disintegrate in Act 2; the ways selfishness is exposed in Act 3

• whether the play is comic, or not – you might consider the ways Griffiths uses the forms and language of jokes; what makes some jokes funny for you, and others not; the fact that Waters never laughs during the play; the fact that he laughs at the end, at a joke containing no stereotypes or aggression

• whether the play is 'about comedy' – you could mention some of the other things that you think the play is 'about'.

There is clearly plenty of material here about the form, structure and language of the play, about the effects of these elements on the audience, and on you, and about the nature of the play. 'To what extent' in the task means that you have to evaluate the views of the play you have explored, and come to your own 'independent judgement'. In the conclusion to the response you could concentrate on the effect of one element, such as the effect of the ending to the play, or the way Griffiths uses mime – to make the audience laugh, in the case of the Caretaker, or to disturb, in the case of Gethin Price's act.

Section B: Poetry

Pre 1900 Poetry

The same Assessment Objectives (AO1, AO2i, AO3, AO5i) are tested in the Pre 1900 Poetry as in the Pre 1900 Drama with Assessment Objective 5i dominant. Remember, if you study a Pre 1900 Poetry text you must also study Modern Drama.

Exploring Pre 1900 Poetry

In this section on Pre 1900 Poetry a number of different contexts will be offered for you to explore:

• the context of period and genre

• historical context

• various social contexts, including religious and moral contexts, and love relationships

• a biographical context.

You will be using skills to study the poetry in this module similar to those you used to look at Pre 1900 Drama. You should ask yourself some of the same questions that you asked about drama:

• what different *contexts* can I find within the poetry?

• how has the writer used *form, structure and language* to convey the ideas and experience within these contexts?

The Canterbury Tales by Geoffrey Chaucer – *The Miller's Tale*

The Canterbury Tales comprises a series of stories told by pilgrims on their journey from London to Canterbury. As these tales were written towards the end of the fourteenth century they fall into the category of medieval literature. In this section you will look at some of the ideas and traditions which provided the context for Chaucer's writings and the influences on his use of language and verse forms.

(As in the Drama section there are several other contexts within the poetry apart from those used as examples in this book. There are also different readings of the text other than those discussed here.)

There will be four contexts considered in this section:

- the social context

- the literary context

- the moral context

- the language context.

The social context

In medieval society there were five estates, or 'classes' of population; at the top, the military or knightly class; then the members of the clergy, and then the commoners; below this were women, and then animals. The Miller is an artisan member of the commoners, (that is to say that he has a craft). He is reasonably well-off, being the miller on a lord's estate, and therefore responsible for collecting the corn which tenants owe their lord. His 'thumbe of gold' suggests this wealth, but also might hint that perhaps the Miller tilts the scales with his thumb to get a little extra corn for himself; so he is rather dishonest.

The Miller is described in the General Prologue, and Chaucer picks out a few significant points about his appearance and attitudes. He has 'blake' and 'wyde' nostrils, which to the medieval mind indicated lust. His mouth is 'as a grete forneys', suggesting maybe that he is loud, talkative and perhaps a liar. As for his temperament, you read that if he cannot tear a door from its hinges, he will 'breke it at a rennyng with his head'; might this suggest violence, clumsiness, and a lack of reason which explains why he so misunderstands his young wife? He can also 'pleye a baggepipe wel'.

ACTIVITY 35

Work through all the characteristics above, and consider what sort of tale you might expect from the Miller. Then read the tale, and discuss how well you think that it is suited to its narrator.

The literary context

At the start of the tale the reader is offered a prologue, which reveals a lot about the genre and the author. This tale about 'harlotrie' is from the genre of fabliau or tales, as opposed to the moral fable told previously by the Knight, for example, and in this way, Chaucer achieves variety in *The Canterbury Tales*.

The prologue to the tale is significant for the way in which Chaucer plays about with literary traditions. Usually, a speaker begins with a plea to the audience for sympathy, and a kindly hearing. But here, Chaucer turns the idea on its head. The Miller is loud and overbearing, says that he is drunk and he appears to be a 'cherl'; so instead of pleading to the audience, he puts on a great show, and insists that he can do better than the Knight:

> I kan a noble tale for the nones,
> With which I wol now quite the Knightes tale.

However, the tone of the prologue is not quite that of a drunken miller; perhaps the voice of the poet comes through as he describes the variety of tales in the collection, adding:

> Blameth nat me if that ye chese amis.
> The Millere is a cherl, ye knowe wel this;

ACTIVITY 36

- Who do you think is speaking here?

- What is being said to the audience? Who is to blame if the tale is offensive?

- Why might it seem necessary to add these lines?

The moral context

Probably the central question to ask here is whether there is a framework of traditional Christian morality. The first thing to think about is the 'sin' of the Miller: he is a fraudster over the corn. But compare this to the sins of other members of the pilgrimage, particularly church officers such as the Pardoner, who corrupt people's eternal souls.

ACTIVITY 37

- How serious a sin is the Miller's. Is it mortal and deadly to the soul, or is it lesser and venial? Remember, Chaucer is not too harsh on the Miller.

- If it is venial, what sort of outcomes might you expect?

There are, of course, references to religion. Alysoun goes to Church on a Saint's Feast Day: and look what happens! She sees the 'joly' Absolon, who 'casts many a lovely look' on the 'wyves' of the Parish, especially Alysoun. He also covers her with incense, so is she one of his gods?

Then we know that there are the bells summoning the friars to lauds, but it has the opposite effect of ending Alysoun and Nicholas's love-play, which began at Curfew.

The carpenter, John knows vaguely of the tale of the flood, but as a distant memory, 'ful yoore ago', and he still believes in witchcraft when he casts his 'nyghtspel' on his house.

References to Christian religion mix freely with references to the pagan Gods, and this fits in with the idea of the fabliau which is linked to Pagan times with its comedy and freedom in displaying the phallus!

Finally, look at the outcomes: do they suggest a Christian scheme of reward and punishment?

Or are they more in keeping with the fun and high spirits of the world of the fabliau?

ACTIVITY 38

To help you decide, think about the outcomes for:

- John: does he deserve what he gets?

- Absolon: what does he learn to avoid? Is it Christian to learn that revenge is sweeter than love?

- Nicholas: is it fair that he can overwhelm the lowly John with the help of his high-and-mighty University chums?

- Alysoun: does she suffer at all?

Isn't the whole tale rather like a child-like fantasy; there was no need for any of the tricks on John, because he was often away staying at Oseney Abbey, and Alysoun needed no persuasion anyway?

The language context

In this section you will consider structure, language and form.

The medieval influence on *The Canterbury Tales* is not just restricted to the ideas but also extends to the structure, where there is a different sort of method of construction at work than is seen today. To understand medieval literature, it might be helpful to understand some of the ideas behind Gothic principles of building. In modern times we tend to expect a logical and clearly sequenced piece of literature. But the medieval mind did not work like this, as you will see in the following picture of Salisbury Cathedral. The building is a mass of different styles: outside there will be those curving, supporting arches, known as flying buttresses, next to intricate carved statues; inside there may be a real mishmash of styles. There will be intricate little statues in niches again, and large statues, delicate filigree designs on the plaster of the walls, and huge soaring plain arches. All the component parts will be different, but the overall effect is of a beautiful and majestic building. This is how the medieval mind worked in Gothic architecture and it was similar in literature. Lots of different effects were interlocked to give a final tapestry-like structure.

ACTIVITY 39

Look at the photographs of the inside and outside of Salisbury Cathedral, and note the different aspects of style that you see.

Chaucer similarly constructed his poetry from a combination of different styles, use of flashbacks and changes of tense, contradictions, a mixture of language from the homely and colloquial to formal literary language, ambiguity, irony, and undercutting. All these elements are **interlaced** to give the final tapestry effect of the poem's form and structure. In *The Miller's Tale* Chaucer interlaces the two plots, the courtship by Absolon and the trick on John with the word 'water'. When Nicholas calls out for water to soothe his burnt backside, the word water links in with the water of Noah's Flood, and the 'gulling' of John.

Chaucer's use of language

Chaucer uses imagery, irony, undercutting and exploits the form of the poem to present really lively central characters.

Imagery: As in any poetry, imagery is important in *The Miller's Tale*. In the descriptions of Alysoun, Chaucer uses many significant images and here is an example:

> She was ful moore blisful on to see
> Than the newe pere-jonette tree,
> And softer than the wolle is of a wether …
> But of hir song, it was as loude and yerne
> As any swalwe sittinge on a berne. …
> She was a primerole, a piggesnie,
> For any lord to leggen in his bedde,
> Or yet for any good yeman to wedde.

ACTIVITY 40

How does Chaucer describe Alysoun here? You might think about these points:

- How does Chaucer use the different senses to describe her, why does he use images of sensuousness, like the touch of soft wool, and why does he describe her liveliness and high spirits? Is he 'placing' her as a 'physical' person, or as a 'spiritual' person?

- How do the references to the Lord and bed help to place Alysoun socially?

- What do all of these effects suggest about her nature and character?

Irony is frequently used in Chaucer's writing. Here is an example from the description of Absolon. This young man is frequently described in feminine terms, with his eyes 'greye as goos', his golden hair, his pretty, high-pitched singing voice, his fondness for giving women 'wafres, pipyng hot out of the gleede'. We also learn that he is very vain: 'In hoses rede he wente fetisly'. But later Chaucer adds another point:

> But sooth to seyn, he was somdeel squaymous
> Of farting, and of speche daungerous.

Absolon also seems to impress Alysoun when 'He playeth Herodes upon a scaffold high'.

ACTIVITY 41

Can you see how Chaucer is sending up Absolon here?

- Herod was a leading part in one of the Mystery plays of the period, *The Slaughter of the Innocents*. It is a very masculine role, a big man with a big voice and lots of charisma. Can you imagine how the high-pitched fellow will appear on stage?

Then think about the comment on his squeamishness and his dislike of farting.

- How might this rebound on him at the end of the tale, with his kissing Alysoun?

In the presentation of Nicholas, you may find other examples of this irony. For example, when Chaucer describes Nicholas's comfortable life he explains that the scholar lives 'After his freendes fyndyng and his reente': he lives without responsibilities. But Chaucer also uses another technique in his description of the scholar.

Undercutting: Chaucer undercuts and undermines a previous statement when he describes Nicholas as 'hende', and 'lyk a maiden meke for to see'. Suddenly he adds that Nicholas is 'sleigh and ful privee', blasting the previous description. Here is another example when he and Alysoun pretend that he is sick, and he stays in his room:

This passeth forth al thilke Saterday,
That Nicholas stille in his chambre lay,
And eet and sleep, or dide what him leste,
Til Sonday, that the sonne gooth to reste.

ACTIVITY 42

Can you pick up little bits of sarcasm here? What does Nicholas actually do most of the time while he is living off his friends? Why might Chaucer say that the sun goes to 'reste': is it a slur on Nicholas, and his love of 'rest'?

Style: the *form* of a considerable part of the *Tales* is that later known as the **heroic couplet**, that is, iambic pentameters rhymed in pairs. Iambic pentameter is a line with five weakly stressed syllables each followed by a strong one; the lines are rhymed in pairs. Here is an example:

And she sproong as a colt dooth in the trave,
And with hir heed she wryed faste awey
And seide, 'I wol nat kisse thee, by my fey!
Why, lat be,' quod she, 'lat be, Nicholas,
Or I wol crie "out, harrow" and "allas"!
Do wey youre handes, for youre curteisie!'

ACTIVITY 43

The important factor is the way that Chaucer varies the stresses to make effects. You might think about:

1 the effects of the rhyme by bringing certain words together

2 how the metre helps to convey meaning

3 how she expresses herself with animal vitality

4 how Chaucer manages to create such a naturalistic effect as the sound of this young woman speaking.

ACTIVITY 44

Using the model above, explore the pattern of stresses in some of the most famous lines of the poem, after Absolon has delivered his kiss:

He felte a thing al rough and long yherd,
And seide, 'Fy! allas! what have I do?'
    'Tehee!' quod she, and clapte the window to,
And Absolon gooth forth a sory pas.

This concludes the section on *The Miller's Tale,* one of the most entertaining texts on this specification; well, it is still pretty rude, even nowadays! You will no doubt expand on all of the examples given above, and will go on to consider other contexts, such as the social context of the role of women in society, and the period contexts of learning and scholarship evident in the tale. This wide range of contexts may also be found in the poetry of Christina Rossetti.

The poetry of Christina Rossetti

Christina Rossetti led a quiet life at home because of her ill-health. She was a strong Christian, a member of the High Anglican Church. Because of this her engagement to a Pre-Raphaelite painter was ended when he turned to Roman Catholicism, and there is a suggestion that she later fell in love with a married man. Not surprisingly, in her poetry there is often a sense of wistfulness, of life having passed her by. Her religious faith is often evident in her writing. However, there was an entirely different element in her life compared to the strictness of her religious belief, and this was due to her brother, Dante Gabriel Rossetti. He was a Pre-Raphaelite painter, famed for the richness and sensuousness of his paintings of women. Sometimes there is strong evidence in her poetry that some of this sensuousness has rubbed off on to her. There is also, at times, a sense of joy in her poetry, and this joy can be due to the love of God, or human love. The first poem to be explored is 'A Birthday', which celebrates the happiness found through love.

AO2i: knowledge and understanding of the poem

This is a poem celebrating human love. It is quite unusual to find such a joyful, carefree tone in Christina Rossetti's poetry, as she is so often sad or resigned or wistful.

AO5i: five contexts are to be explored here

- poems of human love

- poems of fantasy

- poems about nature

- poems about religion

- poems about Christian consolation.

AO5i: the first context to be considered is the context of human love
---

This is a *social context*, but also a *biographical context* as Rossetti herself suffered the pangs of unrequited love.

Her poem 'A Birthday' is a song celebrating love:

> My heart is like a singing bird
>   Whose nest is in a watered shoot;
> My heart is like an apple-tree
>   Whose boughs are bent with thick-set fruit;
> My heart is like a rainbow shell
>   That paddles in a halcyon sea;
> My heart is gladder than all these
>   Because my love is come to me.

Raise me a dais of silk and down;
    Hang it with vair and purple dyes;
Carve it in doves, and pomegranates,
    And peacocks with a hundred eyes;
Work it in gold and silver grapes,
    In leaves, and silver fleurs-de-lys;
Because the birthday of my life
    Is come, my love is come to me.

vair is a decorated fur.
fleurs-de-lys are emblems used in heraldry.

AO3: how the writer expresses ideas related to these contexts

ACTIVITY 45

What does Christina Rossetti have to say about the feeling of being in love in the first stanza? You need to think about:

- the series of pictorial images, such as the bird and the tree and the shell

- the use of repetition and the appeal to all of the senses

- the build-up to the comparison in the last line of this stanza

- the varied rhyme schemes combined with the use of a regular rhythm.

In the second stanza, the poet changes tone and pace. Instead of looking at 'my' love, she describes more objectively the state of being in love.

ACTIVITY 46

How does Christina Rossetti develop her ideas about love in the second stanza of this poem? You need to think about:

- the use of images of queenliness

- the use of texture and of colour

- the use of the senses

- the various meanings of the word 'birthday'.

However, as we all know, there are dangers attached to sexual love, and in her fantasy poems sometimes the dangers of forbidden love can be read into the poems as in 'Goblin Market'.

AO2i: knowledge and understanding of the text

'Goblin Market' is written in the form of an epic poem; this means that it is a long narrative poem telling the story of two sisters Laura and the heroine, Lizzie. Each evening, the goblins tempt young maidens with luscious fruits to buy and to eat. Laura is tempted to do so, and falls ill and is dying. The poem tells of Lizzie's heroic attempt to get hold of this fruit, to resist tasting it herself, and to give the juices to her sister. This cures her sister. The poem is set in the medieval period, rather like Pre-Raphaelite paintings. There are lots of different readings to be read into this poem, but the idea of eating forbidden fruit reminds the reader of the Garden of Eden, where Adam and Eve were expelled for the same thing. Perhaps the forbidden fruit, therefore, could be sexual love. You will form your own views when you have read this strange poem.

AO5i: the context to be explored is the psychological context of fantasy

---

AO3: how the writer expresses ideas related to this context

The idea that the poem may be concerned with the forbidden fruit of sexual love is supported by the very sensuous language used at times. Laura has decided that she will buy the fruit carried by the strange little men, and she eats it. The fruit is described:

> Sweeter than honey from the rock,
> Stronger than man-rejoicing wine,
> Clearer than water flowed that juice;
> She never tasted such before, …

ACTIVITY 47

The fruit is obviously very special, and the description is rich; how does Christina Rossetti create the effects here? You might think about:

- the use of the list of comparisons

- the build-up to the last line quoted and the final statement here

- the use of the senses

- the effects of the **sibilance** and of the word 'never'.

The sheer sensuous pleasure of Laura's 'temptation and fall' is conveyed lusciously; could it be forbidden love? After eating, Laura languishes and will die unless her sister can save her. So Lizzie, her brave sister, faces the goblins but must not eat. The goblins are described as 'lashing their tails': are they dragon-like, or might they be devils? The idea is left open. But Lizzie stands firm:

>   White and golden Lizzie stood,
> Like a lily in a flood, –
> Like a rock of blue veined stone
> Lashed by tides obstreperously, –
> Like a beacon left alone
> In a hoary roaring sea,
> Sending up a golden fire, – …
> Like a royal virgin town …

Lizzie resists and she is pictured very clearly as she confronts the goblins.

ACTIVITY 48

This presentation of the heroine Lizzie reveals quite a lot about Christina Rossetti's mind. It would help if you could look at one of the Pre-Raphaelite paintings, such as those by Christina's brother, Dante Gabriel Rossetti, and his *Astarte Syriaca* or *Veronica Veronese*. Christina Rossetti could be describing the woman in one of his medieval-style pictures. How does she create this picture in words? You might consider:

- the build-up of the picture of the young woman in the list headed by 'like' (this is how a true epic simile works, by extending the image on and on)

- the use of colour

- the contrast of the delicate girl and cruel nature

- importantly, the reference to the 'virgin tower'.

Do you think this last image gives a clue to one reading of the poem?

What you have in this poem is a combination of many elements: the sense of something forbidden: is it sexual love? Is this the influence of the Church? Is it because virginity is socially essential for woman of this period? (Both girls get married at the end of the poem.) Yet there is the highly sensuous, almost erotic language: is this the opposite influence, the heady, exotic world of her brother and the Pre-Raphaelite painters? A similar poem for you to study would be 'Dream Land'.

When you think of two of the major influences on Christina Rossetti, the sensuous world of her brother and the Pre-Raphaelite painters, and at the other end of the spectrum, the High Church of England, and consider the vast difference between them, it is no wonder that her poetry was widely varied in tone. You will see yet another type in the next poem to be considered, 'Spring'.

AO2i: knowledge and understanding of the text

At times she is a keen observer of nature, with a sharp eye for detail, as illustrated in the following extracts from her poem 'Spring'.

AO5i: the contexts to be considered here are those of nature and of religion

Here is the second stanza of the poem:

Blows the thaw-wind pleasantly,
Drips the soaking rain,
By fits looks down the waking sun:
Young grass springs on the plain;
Young leaves clothe early hedgerow trees;
Seeds, and roots, and stones of fruits,
Swollen with sap put forth their shoots;
Curled-headed ferns sprout in the lane;
Birds sing and pair again.

ACTIVITY 49

This is a fresh and vivid picture of a spring awakening, with lots of detail. How has Christina Rossetti achieved effects here? You might think about:

- how she creates such a sense of activity: look at the use of the present tense repeated throughout the poem

- the punctuation; why are there so many end-stopped lines?

- the assonance of 'drips', 'fits', 'springs'

- the list effect in the long line six

- the final harmony in the reference to the birds.

When you look closely at her poetry in this way, you will see that it is technically complex, and is really well controlled. Here is a second extract from the next verse of the poem:

There is no time like Spring,
When life's alive in everything,
Before new nestlings sing,
Before cleft swallows speed their journey back
Along the trackless track –
God guides their wing, …

AO3: how the writer expresses ideas related to these contexts

ACTIVITY 50

What observations does Christina Rossetti make about nature here? You could consider:

- her eye for minute detail

- the use of the birds as images of spring

- the simplicity of the language with its positive connotations

- the sense of celebration of life.

There is obviously another important theme in this extract, that of religion. Rossetti builds up to the idea of God controlling the spring.

ACTIVITY 51

1 What impression do you get of God's guidance in this poem?

2 Do you think that the poem could be more than just a celebration of spring?

Christina Rossetti wrote much religious poetry, and was also concerned with the idea of death. Here are the first and last verses from a poem called 'Up-Hill'. This provides a contrast to the previous poem and is perhaps more like a hymn than a song:

Does the road wind up-hill all the way?
    Yes, to the very end.
Will the day's journey take the whole long day?
    From morn to night, my friend. …

Shall I find comfort, travel-sore and weak?
    Of labour you shall find the sum.
Will there be beds for me and all who seek?
    Yea, beds for all who come.

AO2i: knowledge and understanding of the poem

The poem is **allegorical**, it is about mankind's journey through life to death and salvation, or 'comfort'. The word allegorical suggests that although the poet is talking about a journey, there is another deeper level of meaning implied.

AO5i: the context to be considered is the religious context

AO3: how the writer expresses the ideas related to this context

- The writer uses dialogue to convey her ideas. One voice asks questions, and the second voice answers them. This gives a dramatic feeling to the poem.

- The rhythm varies with each speaker.

- The voice of the first speaker, who asks the questions, is given a four-stressed line, longer than that of the second speaker. This helps to suggest the difficulty of the 'up-hill' journey through life.

  The lines given to the second speaker are shorter, with three stresses, perhaps to suggest the ease felt on arrival.

- The language of the first speaker emphasises the effort: 'up-hill', 'all', 'whole', 'long'; is this why 'up-hill' is a hyphenated word?

- The language is slightly **archaic**, or deliberately old-fashioned, and solemn: 'morn' and 'my friend'.

- This register recalls the language of hymns, as it talks of achieving rest in heaven and establishes the *religious context* of the poem.

ACTIVITY 52

Using the model above, analyse the second stanza in this extract.

Finally, it might be helpful to explore a recurring motif in Christina Rossetti's poetry, which may be seen in the poem 'If Only'.

AO2i: knowledge and understanding of the poem

The poem 'If Only' illustrates the Christian idea of consolation, the idea that there will be a reward in heaven for those who endure some suffering on earth.

AO5i: the context to be explored is the religious context

This poem is loosely a sonnet in form, with two linked sets of four lines, and then a **sestet,** with its concluding couplet. The first four lines set out the theme and mood of the poem:

> If I might only love my God and die!
>   But now He bids me love Him and live on,
>   Now when the bloom of all my life is gone,
> The pleasant half of life has quite gone by. …

AO3: how the writer expresses ideas related to this context

ACTIVITY 53

Read these lines carefully, and think about:

- what the author's main idea is

- what her attitude to God is, and how the tone helps to convey this

- the language – the **alliteration** of 'l' and 'h' and the effect on tone.

In the central part of the poem Christina Rossetti presents life as part of the natural cycle; summer 'glowed and shone', but winter 'frets with its fitful windy sigh', and it 'numbs'. How might these words relate to the writer as well as the seasons?

The last two lines complete the poem and take the ideas in another direction:

>   Yes, they shall wax who now are on the wane,
> Yea, they shall sing for love when Christ shall come.

ACTIVITY 54

Here Christina Rossetti presents the typically Christian consolation of finally finding joy through God. How does she develop this idea in the last two lines? You might think about:

- the sort of mood that is finally established here

- the repetition of 'yes' and the hymn-like 'yea'

- the reference to cycles at the end, where 'wax' replaces the 'wane' of life

- the connotations of 'sing' and of love for Christ.

Here you have seen several characteristics of the religious aspect of Christina Rossetti's poetry. The tone is of quiet acceptance with some final optimism, established through the careful use of language. If you are studying this poetry, it might be interesting to compare this poem with 'One Day', where the idea of a Christian consolation is again used, but in the context possibly of heterosexual love.

The contexts you have looked at in the poetry of Christina Rossetti include those of love, nature and religion, including the idea of Christian consolation. There are, of course, other possible readings of these poems, and other contexts for you to consider, such as the mythical poems like 'Noble Sisters', and poems of local tradition, such as 'Cousin Kate'.

The poetry of Thomas Hardy

In 1895, after the publication of *Jude the Obscure* was met with great hostility, Hardy gave up writing his major fiction, and decided to concentrate on writing poetry. His first collection was printed three years later, although some of the poems had been written considerably earlier.

His poetry is quite unlike his prose fiction. The tone tends to be quiet, resigned to the difficulties of life and to human insignificance in face of eternity. The style tends to be apparently simple, unpretentious in language, and sincere. For these reasons the poetry of Thomas Hardy is generally considered to be effective and moving.

There are several key contexts related to his poetry, including:

- poetry of self-analysis and reflection
- love poetry
- poetry of place
- poetry of nature
- philosophical poetry.

(You may find that these contexts overlap within individual poems.)

Poetry of self-analysis and reflection

'I Look into My Glass' is typical of this group of poems.

> **AO2i: knowledge and understanding of the poem**

This is a moving poem, written as the speaker/poet surveys his aged face in a mirror and thinks about his life.

AO5i: the context is that of human nature, (social) and psychological

Here is the first verse from the poem:

I look into my glass,
And view my wasting skin,
And say, 'Would God it came to pass
My heart had shrunk as thin!'

In the central verse the speaker/poet thinks that if his heart had shrunk, then 'hearts grown cold to me' would cause no distress, and he could calmly wait for death. Then in the final verse the poem continues:

But Time, to make me grieve,
Part steals, lets part abide;
And shakes this fragile frame at eve
With throbbings of noontide.

AO3: how the writer expresses ideas related to these contexts

ACTIVITY 55

Here you are offered a simple idea. The poet/speaker, an old man, realises how aged he has become, but is forced to suffer because he still has moments of passion. It is a quiet poem, simply expressed, and it is therefore really effective as it moves the reader's sympathy. You might think about:

- how this effectiveness is achieved: look at the register of loss and decay

- the language: are the words simple? is there much imagery?

- the tone: how does the plea to God affect you?

- the sort of trick nature has played upon him

- what you make of the contrast between 'fragile form' and 'throbbing' in the third verse

- whether the passion is simply human love: how might it relate to a poet?

Overall, this seems to be a sad and genuine reflection of his feelings; it does not appear to be self-pitying. So, because of its apparent simplicity the poem does seem to affect readers. How do you respond to it? You might compare this to similar poems such as 'In a Eweleaze near Weatherbury'.

Love poetry

Thomas Hardy married Emma Gifford in 1874, a marriage which was ended by her death in 1912. There are suggestions that he might have been kinder to his wife, however his great love poems were a group written in her memory, 'Poems of 1912–13'. Some readers believe that guilt was a motive as much as love; however, many critics consider that these are his best poems. 'The Going' is typical of these poems.

AO2i: knowledge and understanding of the poem

This poem laments the suddenness of his wife's death.

AO5i: the context to be considered is that of love

The poem opens with almost a cry to his wife:

> Why did you give no hint that night
> That quickly after the morrow's dawn,
> And calmly, as if indifferent quite,
> You would close your term here, up and be gone
>   Where I could not follow
>   With wing of swallow
> To gain one glimpse of you ever anon!

This is a very strange sort of love, isn't it? And what has happened to the quiet tone of the previous poem?

AO3: how the writer expresses ideas related to this context

ACTIVITY 56

To unpack the curious mood and twists of this poem, you might think about:

- the tone in which the speaker addresses his loved one

- the fact that there is no question mark, just an exclamation mark: why do you think this is so?

- what exactly he accuses his beloved of: why does he write 'calmly'?

- why the image of a legal contract, 'close your term', is used when it is so impersonal

- the **enjambment** when the speaker talks of the swallows; what effects might this achieve?

If you were to conclude that the speaker is angry, it would seem quite fair; but why?

Is he angry at his beloved, or at himself? As you read further through the poem there might be an exclamation, in the fifth stanza where the speaker says:

> Why, then, latterly did we not speak,
> Did we not think of those days long dead,
> And ere your vanishing strive to seek
> That time's renewal? …

ACTIVITY 57

Perhaps here is the root of the poem. What do you think is going on in the speaker's mind here? You might think about:

- what it is that the speaker is regretting

- the effects of the alliteration on the letter 'd'

- the contrast between 'vanishing' and 'renewal'.

The poem finishes on this note of utter loss, with the slight accusatory tone to the beloved:

> ...O you could not know
> That such swift fleeing
> No soul foreseeing –
> Not even I – would undo me so!

The poem ends as it began, on a cry, a shout of despair; the dashes in the line emphasising the shock. Do you think that the poet has achieved a very powerful, if unusual, account of loss here in his extraordinary love poem? You might continue to explore similar poems such as 'The Voice'.

Poetry of place

Thomas Hardy shows great skills when he describes place, with infinite care and the use of lovely images. An example here would be 'Beeny Cliff'.

AO2i: knowledge and understanding of the text

Thomas Hardy and his wife met near Beeny Cliff, and had many happy times together in North Devon. In this poem Hardy recalls the place carefully, and goes on to associate it with his memories of Emma.

AO5i: the context to be explored here is that of geographical place, although the context of love also applies to this poem
---

> O the opal and the sapphire of that wandering western sea, …
> A little cloud then cloaked us, and there flew an irised rain,
> And the Atlantic dyed its levels with a dull misfeatured stain,
> And then the sun burst out again, and purples prinked the main.

AO3: how the writer expresses the ideas related to the context of nature
---

You will notice at once that we are back to the delicate tone of the first poem explored. Quite clearly, the poet stands on the cliff top and looks down at the 'levels' of the Atlantic Ocean off the coast. How does he make this description so effective?

ACTIVITY 58

You might think about these questions:

- What are the effects created by comparing the colour of the sea to precious or semi-precious stones, the opal and the sapphire?

- Then, later, to the delicate flower, the iris?

- What connotations does the colour purple have?

- Does this remind you of the delicate tones of a watercolour painting? (Thomas Hardy was trained as an architect, and therefore would be able to sketch fairly well.)

If you are studying this poet, then you might go on to consider the *context of love* in this poem.

As you will have seen, Hardy is very delicate in his description of places; you could explore other poems here, such as 'Under the Waterfall'.

Poetry of nature (and philosophical poetry)

This is the final context to be considered in Thomas Hardy's poetry; again, natural details are conveyed with precision, delicacy and great accuracy. The poem to be explored here is 'The Darkling Thrush'.

AO2i: knowledge and understanding of the text

In this lovely, delicate poem Thomas Hardy sees an old thrush; he hears the bird singing, and this makes him think again about his own unhappy state.

AO5i: the context to be explored here is that of nature, although the psychological context of self-analysis is also present

---

Hardy explains in the poem how he is out on a bleak winter's night:

> I leant upon a coppice gate
>   When Frost was spectre-gray,
> And Winter's dregs made desolate
>   The weakening eye of day.
> The tangled bine-stems scored the sky
>   Like strings of broken lyres,
> And all mankind that haunted nigh
>   Had sought their household fires.
>
> ---
> * *bine-stems* are the tangles of a climbing weed.

Hardy seems to catch here the despair and isolation of a winter evening, again in a delicate pen-sketch.

AO3: how the writer presents the context of nature

ACTIVITY 59

How are the effects created here so finely? You might explore:

- the use of colour, or lack of colour in the frost and the sky

- the personification of the frost and winter

- the idea of spirits and ghosts, and human isolation

- the disharmony of broken lyres and the violent verb 'scored'.

What sort of scene and mood is presented here?

Then suddenly, a thrush appears:

An aged thrush, frail, gaunt, and small,
    In blast-beruffled plume,
Had chosen thus to fling his soul
    Upon the growing gloom.

Again, there is a light and delicate touch to the poem, and a tender note, perhaps. How does Hardy create this picture, and manipulate your response to it? You might think about:

- how it is that the thrush appears to be heroic

- the sort of register used to describe him

- whether this register might also apply to the poet (Remember the poem which you looked at earlier, 'I Look into My Glass'.)

- why the poet writes 'to fling his soul'

- how this bird might present a change to the mood of the poem.

You will have noticed how delicate, and almost tender and gentle the description of the bird was. This prepares for the climax of the poem when the writer decides that the bird had some 'blessed hope', of which he himself 'was unaware'. With that little twist the context moves into that of self-analysis, and the resigned disappointment at the ending of the poet's joy in life. There are other poems similar to this, for example, 'The Last Chrysanthemum'.

Perhaps there are two predominant aspects in the poetry of Thomas Hardy which you have studied so far: the first of these is Hardy's eye for detail, and his delicacy in conveying these effects, almost with the skill of a watercolourist.

The second aspect is the way in which contexts within his poems merge into each other; it seems to be rather rare to find a poem with a single context. Maybe this is because at the root of Thomas Hardy's poetry is a concern for the way his life has diminished as he has aged. Then, beyond that, there is the sense of the rather hopeless state of mankind, as the author sees it, in the face of an indifferent universe which dwarfs man. Perhaps the clearest expression of this *philosophical context* is 'The Convergence of the Twain'.

AO2i: knowledge and understanding of the poem

Thomas Hardy presents in this poem the pride of man as the *Titanic* is built; at the same time, an iceberg is forming. You will probably know the story from the film: inevitably, they collide and the ship is lost.

AO5i: the context to be considered here is the philosophical context

The last verse offers Thomas Hardy's viewpoint on what has happened: all goes well:

> Till the Spinner of the Years
> Said 'Now!' And each one hears,
> And consummation comes, and jars two hemispheres.
>
> ---
> * *the Spinner* is a reference to one of the three Greek Goddesses who spun man's destiny for him.

So all the hope and confidence placed in the mighty vessel are reversed.

AO3: how the writer expresses ideas related to this context

ACTIVITY 60

How does Hardy express his views about the frailty of mankind here? You might think about:

* how the Spinner has the power to overturn man's plans

* how urgency is conveyed in the imperative verb

* the effect of the four syllables in 'consummation'

* which two hemispheres have been jarred.

How do you respond to Hardy's viewpoint? Do you think that he is a pessimist or a realist? You could compare this to the poem '1967'.

You might go on to explore other contexts in this poetry, such as the *context of social comment or criticism*. These poems, for example those from *Satires of Circumstance*, are not quite like the other poems already explored. They are sharper, often with a sly sort of humour, as when he describes a vain vicar happy because he knocked out his 'fans', his congregation, with a sermon in the poem 'In Church'; or perhaps rather cynical, when Hardy writes about a widow decking herself out in her mourning clothes 'At the Draper's'. Thomas Hardy has a keen eye and a sharp tongue when he mocks human weaknesses such as vanity, and you will smile at his sly humour.

Such poems are worth looking at, to capture the difference in tone from the more self-reflective or self-revealing poems; they are just a small part of Thomas Hardy's wide range.

Post 1900 Poetry

As explained in the introduction to this Poetry section, four Assessment Objectives are tested in this part of the examination paper. You will have to 'communicate clearly the knowledge and understanding appropriate to literary study using appropriate terminology and accurate and coherent written expression' (AO1), 'respond with knowledge and understanding' (AO2i), 'show detailed understanding of the ways in which writers' choices of form, structure and language shape meanings' (AO3), and 'articulate independent opinions and judgements informed by different interpretations of literary texts by other readers' (AO4). The dominant Assessment Objective in this section is AO4, which carries 10 of the 20 marks available, with the other 10 marks split between the other three objectives. A key consideration is AO3, however, as an understanding of the writers' skills and meanings will form the material for demonstrating AOs 2i and 3, and the basis for arriving at 'independent opinions and judgements'. This section, therefore, will deal with these features first, before going on to consider how you can meet AO4 in the examination.

Form

An obvious feature of form in any poem is rhyme, or variations of it, or no rhyme at all, all of which are deliberate choices. The function of rhyme is to connect things, so full rhyme connects things closely. The effect of connecting things in this way can vary from poem to poem, or within the same poem. Full rhyme might be used to establish a sense of certainty, of things belonging. Here are two lines from U. A. Fanthorpe's 'Under the Motorway':

Petrol and diesel will both dry up
But that doesn't happen to a Buttercup.

In the poem the writer suggests that what 'lies in wait' when the motor car has had its day is 'seeds'. The certainty of this is shaped by the sureness of 'doesn't happen', by arranging the sentence so that an end-stopped line after 'Buttercup' ends it, and by the full rhyme, underlined by the stop.

ACTIVITY 61

Read the last two lines from the poem:

Rolls Royce and Volvo, their day is done,
But Charlock and Dandelion blaze in the sun.

1   How is certainty suggested here? Think about the capital letters, the effect of the word 'blaze', and the rhyme.

2   Why are these two words ('done' and 'sun') linked at the end of the poem, which is about flowers lasting?

Here is 'Mrs Icarus' by Carol Ann Duffy:

I'm not the first or the last
to stand on a hillock,
watching the man she married
prove to the world
he's a total, utter, absolute, Grade A pillock.

The only rhyme here is a full rhyme, 'hillock' with 'pillock'. The rhyme draws attention to itself in this way, and by the second rhymed word being the last one of the poem. The comic effect of the last line is created by the last word itself, by the run of adjectives up to it, and by the full rhyme, which underlines the sense of final judgement – he really is a 'pillock'.

Here is the first verse of 'Cut Grass' by Philip Larkin:

Cut grass lies frail:
Brief is the breath
Mown stalks exhale.
Long, long the death

ACTIVITY 62

There are only fifteen words here, but the ideas are connected cleverly through the associations of the words, and the rhymes.

1 The last word of the first line is 'frail'. Which word in the second line has a similar meaning?

2 How do the first and last words of the second line connect? Think about the sound of the words as well as meaning.

3 Now – how does the last word of the third line connect with the last words of the previous two lines?

4 How does the last word of the verse connect with the last words of all the previous lines? Think about sound and meaning.

5 How does Larkin make the death seem long and drawn out? Think about the device in line 4, and the contrasts with line 2.

Rhyme, and forms of rhyme, are often varied for effect. In 'Salome' Carol Ann Duffy introduces the word 'matter' in line 5, and comes back to the sound and shape of this word many times (in fact, it has already been anticipated by 'later' at the end of line 3). Some of the words are full rhymes, such as 'flatter', 'clatter', and 'patter', and some are **half-rhymes** or echoes, such as 'laughter', 'pewter', and 'slaughter'. All of these reinforce the finality of the last line, and the last image, as the rhymes reach this conclusion:

> … his head on a platter.

Here is the third verse of 'Medusa' by Carol Ann Duffy:

> Be terrified.
> It's you I love,
> perfect man, Greek God, my own;
> but I know you'll go, betray me, stray
> from home.
> So better by far for me if you were stone.

ACTIVITY 63

Find all the rhymes and half-rhymes in this verse, looking for rhymes within the lines as well as for rhymes at the end of lines. How do these rhymes gather to 'stone', and what is the effect of this as the last word of the verse?

Variations in form often occur at the end of poems for particular effects. Both 'The Building' and 'The Explosion' by Philip Larkin end with single lines, after verses with a regular number of rhymes. 'The Building' ends with the line:

> With wasteful, weak, propitiatory flowers.

perhaps emphasising the solitary hopelessness of each person's wish not to die. 'The Explosion' ends:

> One showing the eggs unbroken.

creating a single image of something fragile, and not broken, which is suddenly cut off, perhaps – like the verse (where are the other two lines?), and the men's lives.

Overleaf is the end of 'Medusa' by Carol Ann Duffy. In Greek mythology, the Gorgons were three sisters whose faces were so ugly that if men looked on them they were turned to stone. Medusa, whose hair was formed of serpents, was the only mortal Gorgon. She was eventually killed by Perseus; when he came to her for the last time, he came with a sword and shield.

And here you come
with a shield for a heart
and a sword for a tongue
and your girls, your girls.
Wasn't I beautiful?
Wasn't I fragrant and young?

Look at me now.

ACTIVITY 64

1 How does Duffy use metaphor to establish Perseus's attitude to Medusa?

2 How does Duffy establish Medusa's jealousy?

3 What do the two questions tell you about Medusa's feelings?

4 How can the last line be taken in two ways? Think about the questions, and the story.

5 All the preceding verses have five or six lines. How is it appropriate and effective to finish the poem with this single line?

In Philip Larkin's 'The Old Fools', the last line works in a different way. The poem, which is about senility, ends:

Can they never tell
What is dragging them back, and how it will end? Not at night?
Not when the strangers come? Never, throughout
The whole hideous inverted childhood? Well,
We shall find out.

Each verse of this poem is regular, in that it has twelve lines, the last of which is short, as here. The reason for this choice of form is clear here: after the succession of questions, the final four words, isolated as a last line, give the reader a final and horrible answer, personalised by the use of 'we' to start the line.

Here is the end of 'Mrs Quasimodo' by Carol Ann Duffy. Mrs Quasimodo has always loved the bells of the cathedral but, feeling betrayed by Quasimodo, has cut away the clappers from the great bells.

I sawed and pulled and hacked.
I wanted silence back.

Get this:

When I was done,
and bloody to the wrist,
I squatted down among the murdered music of the bells
and pissed.

ACTIVITY 65

1 How does the poet convey Mrs Quasimodo's determination in the first two lines here? Think about the verbs and the rhyme, and the punctuation.

2 Why do you think the poet has chosen to insert a line break after the short line, 'Get this:'?

3 What is the effect of the last line? Think about why the rhymes lead to it, and the effect of the previous long line.

In the quotation from 'Mrs Quasimodo' above, an effect is created by using a break in the text. The lengths of lines (as in the last two lines of 'Mrs Quasimodo') and the positioning of line and verse breaks can be used to create effects. Look at the last eight lines of 'Sad Steps' by Philip Larkin:

Lozenge of love! Medallion of art!
O wolves of memory! Immensements! No,

One shivers slightly, looking up there.
The hardness and the brightness and the plain
Far-reaching singleness of that wide stare

Is a reminder of the strength and pain
Of being young; that it can't come again,
But is for others undiminished somewhere.

'No' is at the end of a line, creating a denial which is doubled by the verse break that follows – the pause the reader is bound to make is lengthened, isolating and emphasising the single word 'No' that starts the sentence. The exaggerated exclamations in the first two lines are undercut by the stop that this makes, and by 'one' and 'slightly' in the next line, which is end-stopped – the whole movement stops at the full stop here. The size of the moon is suggested by the stretching out of the next line ('and the ... and the ...'), and the breaks after 'plain' and 'stare', especially as there is a verse break between 'wide stare' and 'Is ...'. The last sentence, in fact, stretches over five lines and two verses.

Here are the opening ten lines of 'To the Sea' by Philip Larkin:

> To step over the low wall that divides
> Road from concrete walk above the shore
> Brings sharply back something known long before –
> The miniature gaiety of seasides.
> Everything crowds under the low horizon:
> Steep beach, blue water, towels, red bathing caps,
> The small hushed waves' repeated fresh collapse
> Up the warm yellow sand, and further off
> A white steamer stuck in the afternoon –
>
> Still going on, all of it, still going on!

ACTIVITY 66

Look at the ends and beginnings of all the lines here, many of which create effects. Look at the two dashes and the colon, too – what effects do these have? Think particularly about the verse break – what does 'all of it' in the last line refer to, and how does the gap created by the verse break help the effect?

Another feature of form is the creation of voices within poems. Philip Larkin uses this device frequently, for different purposes. In 'Sympathy in White Major', for instance, the narrator of the poem imagines the voices of people who talk about him:

> I lift the lot in private pledge:
> *He devoted his life to others.*

In 'The Room Where Everyone Goes' for instance, Fanthorpe italicises '*Ooh, look! The loo/the toilet/the bog*' to suggest the voices of sundry visitors, while '*Despatched by the hand of God*', presented in the same way, suggests both the diction and the evasiveness of the 'careful cleric'. Carol Ann Duffy creates voices within poems too, and often manufactures a sort of dialogue between the voice of the speaker of the poem and the voice the speaker hears, as in 'Mrs Aesop':

> *Slow*
> *but certain, Mrs Aesop, wins the race.* Asshole.

Here is the opening verse of 'Vers de Société' by Philip Larkin:

My wife and I have asked a crowd of craps
To come and waste their time and ours: perhaps
You'd care to join us? In a pig's arse, friend.
Day comes to an end.
The gas fire breathes, the trees are darkly swayed.
And so *Dear Warlock-Williams: I'm afraid* –

ACTIVITY 67

1 The first 'voice' here is created by italics, and is the beginning of an imagined letter to the speaker of the poem. How do you know that this is an imagined 'typical' letter of invitation, and not a real one?

2 There are two voices of the speaker shown – the mental reply to the letter, and the beginning of the actual reply, again shown in italics. How do these verses contrast, and what does the contrast suggest about the speaker?

Many poems make use of a created **persona**. The use of a narrative 'I' might indicate the poet speaking directly to the reader, or an invented person. If you're studying Philip Larkin, for instance, it would be very tempting to think that the self-deprecating, rather melancholy voice in many of the poems is that of the poet – but is it always? On the other hand, it's perfectly clear that many of the voices created by U. A. Fanthorpe are not hers, as she 'speaks' as foxes, a fairy, and a cat, for example.

A created persona will often seek to show an understanding of the world seen from this person's angle, and to make the reader reflect on the speaker too. Here is the second stanza of Fanthorpe's 'The Invitation', where the voice is that of 'The Gloucestershire foxes':

Us knows the pack be after thee,
Us knows how that du end,
The chase, the kill, the cheering,
Dying wi'out a friend.

The dialect grammar and spelling here, and the sounds created by accent, are important parts of the voice, suggesting rural simplicity, but a simplicity which can speak directly to the child. The hunting, though, makes the reader think about the persecution of both participants, the foxes and Jesus. Further on in the poem, it is men who are referred to as 'beastly', a deliberately ambiguous word which makes the reader consider the nature of man.

Each of the poems in Carol Ann Duffy's *The World's Wife* creates a persona – this is the premise for the collection. In these poems, language is used to establish character, so this will be dealt with below.

Structure

In relatively short literary texts, like the poems in *High Windows* and *The World's Wife*, openings and endings take on particular importance, in terms of the way they shape meanings. The opening to Fanthorpe's 'The Wicked Fairy at the Manger' is very direct: 'My gift for the child:', on an isolated line, followed by a line space, creates an immediate context and voice.

'*Right*, said the baby. *That was roughly/What we had in mind*' is an apparently sudden shift at the end of Fanthorpe's 'The Wicked Fairy', which makes the reader consider the baby, the fairy, and the meaning of the Christmas story. Similarly, 'When thou tires of humanity' at the end of 'The Invitation' startles with the unusual word 'humanity' (unusual for the foxes), and jolts the reader into a reconsideration of meaning.

The opening of 'Vers de Société', quoted on page 167, also establishes a voice in the imaginary letter, and in this poem the ending forms the reply, as the last line is:

> *Dear Warlock-Williams: Why, of course –*

This is a structural choice which completes the line of thought in the poem.

Here are the first four and the last four lines of 'Demeter' by Carol Ann Duffy:

> Where I lived – winter and hard earth.
> I sat in my cold stone room
> choosing tough words, granite, flint,
>
> to break the ice.

and

>   I swear
> the air softened and warmed as she moved,
>
> the blue sky smiling, none too soon,
> with the small shy mouth of a new moon.

ACTIVITY 68

The poem 'Demeter' moves from winter to spring. Pick out all the ways that you can find in which the ending contrasts directly with the beginning. Think about words that suggest:

- temperature

- hardness

- feel

- movement

- colour

- attitude.

The full rhyme in the last two lines is the only rhyme in the poem. Why do you think the poet has made this choice?

Poets often structure their work as a movement from the particular to the universal. 'Sad Steps' by Philip Larkin, for example, begins:

Groping back to bed after a piss
I part thick curtains, …

but ends as shown on page 165 above. By the last verse, the thought has moved from a particular prosaic moment to a thought about 'the strength and pain/Of being young'. The last verse of 'This Be The Verse' begins with a grim thought about life, and an equally grim lesson:

Man hands on misery to man.
  It deepens like a coastal shelf.
Get out as early as you can,
  And don't have any kids yourself.

Another structural framework is movement through time, as in 'To the Sea'. In the opening, quoted on page 166 above, the time is the present, but is referring to the past. In the poem, the speaker thinks about his own past, then returns to the present, and finally draws some universal lessons about the things he sees, which are also timeless:

helping the old, too, as they ought.

'Show Saturday' by Philip Larkin describes the people and activities at a country show, and finally the return home. Here is the ending:

> Back now, all of them, to their local lives:
> To names on vans, and business calendars
> Hung up in kitchens; back to loud occasions
> In the Corn Exchange, to market days in bars,
> To winter coming, as the dismantled Show
> Itself dies back into the area of work.
> Let it stay hidden there like strength, below
> Sale-bills and swindling; something people do,
> Not noticing how time's rolling smithy-smoke
> Shadows much greater gestures; something they share
> That breaks ancestrally each year into
> Regenerate union. Let it always be there.

ACTIVITY 69

1 In the first six lines here, what reminders of time passing are mentioned?

2 What suggestions are there of things coming to an end?

3 In the last six lines, what reminders of time passing are mentioned?

4 Identify the word which suggests rebirth. What choice does the poet make which emphasises the word?

5 There are suggestions here that something important lies behind what these people do, and that they don't realise its importance. Which words and phrases suggest these ideas?

6 Which words suggest that something binds these people together?

7 What is the mood of these lines? Look at the way they begin and end – and think about time again, too.

Language

Verb and sentence forms are choices of language which help to shape meaning. In the quotation from 'Show Saturday' above, for example, 'Let it' is a command, underlined by being used twice in the last six lines. It is an injunction of hope on the behalf of the speaker, and the only time this form is used in the poem.

Here are seven lines from 'The Building' by Philip Larkin:

> See the time,
> Half-past eleven on a working day,
> And these picked out of it; see, as they climb
> To their appointed levels, how their eyes
> Go to each other, guessing; on the way
> Someone's wheeled past, in washed-to-rags ward clothes:
> They see him, too. They're quiet.

ACTIVITY 70

1 What type of sentence is the first one here? Think about the first word.

2 What effect is created by the repetition of 'see' in the first three lines? Think about what the reader is invited to do.

3 What effect is created by 'They see him, too. They're quiet'? Remember your response to question 2.

Exclamations and questions are other forms of sentence that can be used for effect. The exclamations in 'Sad Steps', for example, quoted on page 165 above, establish a frame of mind about the moon which is then undercut and almost mocked. The string of questions at the end of 'The Old Fools' (see page 164 above) serve as a prelude to the horrible certainty of the statement at the end. The pronouns change here for effect, too: the poem is dominated by 'they' and 'you', but 'we' is only used twice, and the change to 'we' at the beginning of the short last line personalises the message for the reader. In the same way, in the middle of 'The Building' the change from the impersonal description of what 'they' are doing to 'we' suddenly personalises the argument for the reader, who has already been drawn into the poem (see above):

> A touching dream to which we all are lulled
> But wake from separately.

Repetitions and lists can also be used to create effects. 'Eurydice' by Carol Ann Duffy, for example, is a poem which moves quickly from the beginning, full of short lines, and quick shifts of rhyme and word play. Almost at the end, though, Eurydice deliberately tempts Orpheus to turn round by flattering him, knowing that if he does so she will be released back to death:

> He was smiling modestly
> when he turned,
> when he turned and he looked at me.

The repetition of the phrase here, especially as the first is isolated in a line by itself, slows the pace and underlines the drama of the moment.

'Show Saturday' by Philip Larkin uses repetitions and lists to create the sense of the variety of the show, and to comment on it:

> four brown eggs, four white eggs,
> Four plain scones, four dropped scones, pure excellences that enclose
> A recession of skills. And, after them, lambing-sticks, rugs,
> Needlework, knitted caps, baskets, all worthy, all well done,
> But less than the honeycombs.

The list of eggs and scones creates a sense of number and balance by the list, the repetitions of words and shape of phrase, and the rhythm of the lines. The same sense of balance appears in 'all worthy, all well done', and at the end of each of the sentences the poet generalises about the significance of the list.

Here are the last six lines of the third part of 'The Devil's Wife' by Carol Ann Duffy, which concerns the crimes, trial and imprisonment of a figure based on Myra Hindley:

> I said Not fair not right not on not true
> not like that. Didn't see didn't know didn't hear.
> Maybe this maybe that not sure not certain maybe.
> Can't remember no idea it was him it was him.
>
> Can't remember no idea not in the room.
> No idea can't remember not in the room.

ACTIVITY 71

Look at all the repetitions of words and phrases, and the shapes of phrases. Look at all the negatives, too, and the lack of punctuation within the sentences. Taken together, what effects do you think these devices create?

The phrase 'it is all right' is repeated several times in Larkin's 'Homage to a Government'. Partly this creates a lukewarm approval, which taken with the 'homage' in the title sets up a clear disapproval; but partly the language creates a voice – a deliberately ordinary one here.

Poets are fond of using unusual or even invented words for effect. U. A. Fanthorpe, for instance, uses the word 'widdershins', an archaic word meaning left-handed, or in a strange way, in 'The Silence' to suggest the ancient writers of the words on the slate. Similarly, Duffy uses the archaic word 'trow,' meaning think, or believe, in 'Beachcomber' to capture the narrator's effort to go back in memory to an earlier time.

Words can be used to suggest things, by playing on ideas and associations. The last line of Fanthorpe's 'The Room Where Everyone Goes' is:

> The scent of the commonplace brings them home.

'Scent', ironically refers to the smell of the toilet, and 'the commonplace' is ambiguous – it means both 'the ordinary' and the common place, i.e. the place which is common to everybody, in any time period, and in any 'home'. Here it could mean 'brings the past back to life', perhaps.

ACTIVITY 72

In 'Sirensong' Fanthorpe describes the sound of enemy bombers above the house in the war:

> The house fluttered,
> As trespassing aircraft droned life-long overhead,

What do you think 'life-long' might mean or imply here? Think about time, the listener's perception of time, and what might happen. The moment is described by an older person looking back, too, which might suggest a further meaning.

The word 'fluttered' is a **personification**. What might the poet be suggesting by using the word 'fluttered'? Think about the house and its occupants.

Playing with words also means playing with the readers' expectations as language unfolds. At the beginning of 'Queening It', Fanthorpe writes:

> Inside every man there lurks the Widow Twankey,
> Brazen and bosomed as a figurehead,
> Dressed to the tens, …

The opening five words suggest something quite serious or heroic, so that 'The Widow Twankey' comes as a shock, and a ludicrous one. 'As a figurehead' suggests something monumental, overpainted and sticking out at the front. 'Dressed to the tens' continues the 'over the top' idea, but 'tens' still comes as a surprise; Fanthorpe uses and changes the cliché of 'dressed to the nines' to humorous effect.

Different language registers can be used to create effects within the same poem. Both 'This Be The Verse' and 'Sad Steps' begin with colloquial, casual language:

'They fuck you up, your mum and dad'

and

'Groping back to bed after a piss'

They move, however, to thoughts about life, seriously expressed:

Man hands on misery to man.
   It deepens like a coastal shelf.

and

Is a reminder of the strength and pain
Of being young; that it can't come again,
But is for others undiminished somewhere.

Just as in prose or drama, a first person poem might contain language which establishes the voice of a character by the use of appropriate words, phrases and sentence forms. In 'Eurydice' by Carol Ann Duffy, the speaker speaks of being:

Eurydice, Orpheus' wife –
to be trapped in his images, metaphors, similes,
octaves and sextets, **quatrains** and couplets,
elegies, limericks, villanelles,
histories, myths …

The language that she feels 'trapped' by is the language of poetry, of course.

Here are some lines from 'Anne Hathaway' by Carol Ann Duffy:

My lover's words
were shooting stars which fell to earth as kisses
on these lips; my body now a softer rhyme
to his, now echo, assonance; his touch
a verb dancing in the centre of a noun.

ACTIVITY 73

1   Which words here are appropriate for the widow of Shakespeare?

2   Work out exactly what you think each of the metaphors might mean here.

3   What is Anne Hathaway's attitude to Shakespeare in these lines, and how do you know?

Sometimes particular types of colloquial language are used to establish character. 'Elvis's Twin Sister', by Carol Ann Duffy, for example, begins 'In the convent, y'all', establishing a Southern states drawl. 'Digs' in the Reverend Mother 'digs the way I move my hips' is 1950s rock 'n' roll language, while 'Lawdy' in the last verse is again Southern states, but given a humorous edge by the setting of the poem – in a convent.

Here is the opening of 'The Kray Sisters' by Carol Ann Duffy:

There go the twins! geezers would say
when we walked down the frog and toad
in our Savile Row whistle and flutes, tailored
to flatter our thr'penny bits, which were big,
like our East End hearts.

ACTIVITY 74

How does the poet establish character in these lines? What is the tone of these lines, do you think, and how is it established?

Carol Ann Duffy is playing with words in the extract above. Elsewhere in *The World's Wife* she plays with common phrases and clichés. In 'Mrs Midas', for instance, the line:

Look, we all have wishes; granted.

is clearly a play on words, using punctuation to make the point. The idea of 'Mrs Aesop' is that Aesop's wife is driven to distraction by his endless search for fables and morals:

                                        Dead men,
Mrs Aesop, he'd say, *tell no tales.* Well, let me tell you now
that the bird in his hand shat on his sleeve,
never mind the two worth less in the bush. Tedious.

Mrs Aesop tells her own 'tale', in which she uses the crude word 'shat' to mock her husband's portentous words. The last word, 'Tedious', as the final single word of an end-stopped line, abruptly mocks the moral too, especially because of the immediate echo of 'bush'.

The sounds of words are a vital ingredient of poetry; many poems are written to be read aloud, and even if they're not, or you're not in a situation where they can be read aloud, you should hear them in your head. They are a key element in shaping meaning.

Look again at the beginning and ending of 'Demeter', printed on page 168 above. At the beginning, the words are wintry – hard 'I' vowels in 'lived', 'winter', 'granite' and 'flint', and five 't' sounds in the first three lines. At the end, to match the 'smiling' spring, the sounds are soft and long – seven 's' sounds in the last three lines, and six round 'o' sounds.

Here is the last verse of 'The Trees' by Philip Larkin:

> Yet still the unresting castles thresh
> In fullgrown thickness every May.
> Last year is dead, they seem to say,
> Begin afresh, afresh, afresh.

ACTIVITY 75

1   Which words in the first two lines suggest growth and movement? Which words suggest the shape of the trees?

2   How does the word (and the idea) 'dead' in the third line contrast with the words and ideas in the first two lines?

3   Growth, movement and life replacing death are established in the first three lines. How are these ideas reinforced in the last line? Think about:

   • the meanings of the words

   • the effect of the repetition

   • the effects of the rhymes

   • the repeated sounds of the last line – and the wind.

Irony depends on word play and association. A clear example is the title of Fanthorpe's 'Christmas Presents'. The 'present' is not gold, but the presentation of a future beyond the present; but more grimly, Christmas presents, or brings, death to the inhabitant of the bed next to the narrator's.

ACTIVITY 76

Here's an example of U. A. Fanthorpe playing with the language of literature in 'Painter and Poet'. She compares the two artists:

> Having only
> Himself to please, he tinkers at pleasing himself.
> Watch silently now as that metaphor
> Fans slowly out, like a fin from the sea.
> Did you notice him then, secret and shy as an otter,
> Transferring an epithet? See that artless adverb
> Mature into a pun!

1 How does the poet play with words in the first sentence?

2 Look at the phrase the 'metaphor fans'. What part of speech is the word 'fans', in fact?

3 The echo of fans/fins makes a connection. But what sort of figure of speech is 'like a fin from the sea'?

4 How is the idea of something coming from the sea continued, and in what figure of speech?

The play on words introduces the idea of 'a pun', although Fanthorpe doesn't give the reader one, just when it's expected.

Most poets use imagery as a way of shaping meanings for readers. Images are effective when they make the reader understand something clearly – so in Carol Ann Duffy's 'Queen Herod', for instance, the simile:

> *a new star*
> *pierced through the night like a nail.*

makes the reader think of Christ's birth, but also of the crucifixion. In 'Mrs Lazarus', the risen Lazarus is described as:

> moist and dishevelled from the grave's slack chew,

The rather grisly metaphor of the grave as a mouth works exactly here – Mrs Lazarus seems horrified by her husband 'in his rotting shroud', and he is beginning slowly to decompose – the chew is 'slack', after all.

A metaphor can often be extended for effect, as in 'The Old Fools' by Philip Larkin:

and them crouching below
Extinction's alp, the old fools, never perceiving
How near it is. This must be what keeps them quiet:
The peak that stays in view wherever we go
For them is rising ground.

The idea of death as an 'alp' lets the writer communicate the idea of something close, frightening and huge – so huge that it can't be seen when really close up to it.

Here is 'Solar' by Philip Larkin, a poem full of imagery:

Suspended lion face
Spilling at the centre
Of an unfurnished sky
How still you stand,
And how unaided
Single stalkless flower
You pour unrecompensed.

The eye sees you
Simplified by distance
Into an origin,
Your petalled head of flames
Continuously exploding.
Heat is the echo of your
Gold.

Coined there among
Lonely horizontals
You exist openly.
Our needs hourly
Climb and return like angels.
Unclosing like a hand,
You give for ever.

ACTIVITY 77

1 Work out all the different things the sun is compared to.

2 Work out how each comparison works – the sun is described as a 'petalled head of flames', for instance, because the flames make it look like the head of a flower. Notice that the words which form comparisons are not always verbs – 'petalled', for instance, and 'Coined'.

3 Think why each comparison might be appropriate for the sun.

At the end of Fanthorpe's 'Dying Fall', the poet refuses to celebrate war:

> Skulls, tongueless bells, miming their message,
> Waiting for the wind to say.

Skulls are like bells in shape, and both have tongues, which gives the poet the opportunity to shape the end of the poem. These skulls have no tongues, suggesting decomposition, perhaps, so their message has to be 'mimed' – they speak wordlessly; it is their appearance which conveys the message. Grimly, the wind will 'say' – a personification, suggesting that the message lies in the leaves blown into the gutter, and the mud. Death, in other words.

ACTIVITY 78

Fanthorpe's 'Atlas' is about the strength of a particular kind of love. Read the last stanza:

> And maintenance is the sensible side of love,
> Which knows what time and weather are doing
> To my brickwork; insulates my faulty wiring;
> Laughs at my dryrotten jokes; remembers
> My need for gloss and grouting; which keeps
> My suspect edifice upright in air,
> As Atlas did the sky.

The whole stanza is built on the comparison between the speaker and a house.

1 Work out all the comparisons, and what the speaker's partner is actually doing, then reflect on how this 'maintenance' is 'the sensible side of love'.

2 The comparison in the last line is different, though: Atlas wasn't a builder, after all. What does this comparison tell you about the partner, and the speaker's attitude to the partner?

AO4: articulate independent opinions and judgements informed by different interpretations of literary texts by other readers

---

This is the dominant Assessment Objective on the twentieth-century texts on this paper, carrying 10 of the 20 marks available. The questions are likely to give a view of the text and the writer, and ask for your opinion. Before considering how you might form a response, it's worth thinking about what the subjects of the questions might be. Broadly, they could focus on the poet's concerns, and how the poet conveys them; the poet's techniques; or the qualities of the poet's work. As an example, here's a list of some of the things which could form the focus of questions about Fanthorpe, Larkin and Duffy. This is not an exhaustive list, by any means, just some examples.

Fanthorpe

- giving voices to those without voices
- using the past to reflect on the present
- war
- the meaning of Christmas
- wit/word play
- love
- houses
- first-person poems: the creation of personae.

Larkin

- nostalgia
- the decline of England
- the approach of old age and death
- the fear of/effect of death
- experience bringing disillusionment/regret
- pressure of society on the individual
- how Larkin conveys hope and youth
- nature
- the ways Larkin creates and uses voices
- the ways Larkin uses **parody**
- moving from specific experience or thoughts to the universal
- the ways Larkin uses different verse forms.

Duffy

- attitudes to men in poems
- presentation of love/sex
- presentation of dislike/hatred/contempt
- use of characters from history/mythology/literature
- effect of transferring old tales to modern contexts
- creation of personae

- use of language/word play

- use of form for effect

- ways of creating comic effects.

Forming a response

As an example, let's suppose that you were studying Duffy, and that the question you were going to tackle was:

'How far do you feel that Carol Ann Duffy's presentation of men in The World's Wife *is unrelentingly negative?'*

You know that:

- you have to consider the view offered

- you have to write about form, structure and language, not just meanings – the word 'exploration' suggests it anyway

- you must reach an 'independent opinion'.

First of all, what material would you use? To consider how this view could be supported, you might want to think about poems like 'Little Red-Cap', 'Mrs Tiresias', 'Mrs Aesop', 'Mrs Darwin', 'Mrs Icarus', 'Mrs Quasimodo', 'Eurydice', 'Medusa' and 'Penelope', and choose ones where you can consider technique as well as ideas. 'Penelope' and' Medusa', for instance, are both structured towards a final condemnation of the men in the poems in some way. The two short poems, 'Mrs Icarus' and 'Mrs Darwin' offer a different type of presentation of the same viewpoint, in that they are essentially comic, and rely for effect on a gag in the last line, sharpened by rhyme and line length.

You might then think about an opposing view, using perhaps 'Anne Hathaway', both for its view of Shakespeare, 'my living laughing love', and for the ways that form, language and structure combine in this poem to shape Anne's voice and attitude. 'Queen Kong' would also offer another view here, and one where the situation and tone are very different from 'Anne Hathaway'.

With some material in mind, you would then go about structuring a response, keeping the critic's view firmly in mind. You should look to develop and qualify your arguments, too; here, for instance, you could take into account that Mrs Midas attacks her husband's idiocy, greed and selfishness, but ends not on this, but on 'I miss most ... his touch'. Pilate's Wife is contemptuous of her husband, but noted that Christ's eyes 'were ... to die for'. Delilah's view of Samson is ambivalent, to say the least. To conclude, your personal view must be evident, and it must be clear that you have reached the judgement *'informed by different interpretations of literary texts by other readers'*.

Summary

This concludes the section on Pre 1900 and Post 1900 poetry. You have seen how contexts and the writers' ways of expressing ideas related to these contexts are logically linked and you have become aware of the great variety of contexts. You have had some practice in evaluating both the ideas behind the literature and the ways in which the writers' choices of form, structure and language shape meanings.

So you now have the necessary 'knowledge and understanding' to help you prepare for your examination in this module.

Revision

As the examinations for your modules get closer, you will need to think about revision, and how you can set about it in a focused way. There are two important elements you need to think about: acquiring knowledge, and thinking about the Assessment Objectives for the questions on the paper.

Knowledge

Whatever you write in the exams on set texts, you'll need to demonstrate your knowledge by supporting your views with quotations from the text, echoes of the texts, details of the text. There are no short cuts here, and no substitute for re-reading the text several times. After all, at each reading you don't simply remember more of it, you also add to your store of understanding, as more and more of the way the text works is revealed to you. It's impossible to understand a text fully from one reading. It would be nice to think that you could, but you can't.

If you read your texts often enough, there'll be no problem in providing good support for what you want to say about the text in response to the exam question. There's no point in 'learning the best 15 quotations to use' – you don't know what the 'best' material is until you see the question. The evidence you should use is *appropriate* evidence.

The examination for Module 1 could well be the first time you've taken a closed book exam in English Literature, and you might find this worrying – but you shouldn't. Having the text with you is only to allow 'open book' style questions – ones which ask you to re-examine carefully a section of the text or to use a given extract as a starting point for discussion. Its purpose isn't to provide knowledge after all, you can't start reading the book in the exam and you won't have the time to start looking things up. Looked at this way, there's no real difference between open and closed book exams.

Assessment Objectives

The focus of this whole book has been on the Assessment Objectives for your course in English Literature, and now isn't the time to forget about them. Your revision should revolve around a consideration of the Assessment Objectives you'll be tested on for each text, so you need to look for and explore these within the text. Of course, this means revisiting the work you've done in and outside class, but it's also where the focus of your re-readings should be.

To help you revise the Assessment Objectives, here's an exercise on them, and how they are used to read a text. Overleaf is an extract from the play *The Steamie* by Tony Roper. 'Steamies' were communal laundries in Glasgow.

MAGRIT	. . . Apart fae you dae mean?
ANDY	Cause. [*Glasgow drunk's hand-signals.*] Zat what ah'm here for . . . now then . . . Z'ivrything awright?
MAGRIT	[*this speech should be done with heavy irony to the audience as she sings 'Isn't it wonderful to be a woman'*] Isn't it wonderful tae be a woman. Ye get up at the crack o' dawn and get the breakfast oan, get the weans ready and oot the hoose lookin' as tidy and as well dressed as ye can afford. Then ye see tae the lord high provider and get him oot, then wash up, finish the ironin', tidy the hoose and gie the flair a skite o'er. Then it's oot tae yer ain wee job, mebbe cleanin' offices, servin' in a shop or washin' stairs. Then it's dinner time. Well it is fur everybody else but no us 'cause we don't get dinner. By the time yer oot and run home, cooked something for the weans, yer lucky if you feel like something tae eat. I know I don't and even if I did . . . the dinner hour's finished, so it's back tae yer work; that is efter ye've goat in whatever yer gonnae gie them for their tea, and efter yer finished yer work, ye'r back up . . . cookin' again and they'll tell ye the mince is lumpy . . . or the chips are too warm . . . then they're away oot. The weans tae play . . . the men tae have a drink, cause they need wan . . . the souls . . . efter pittin' in a hard day's graft, so ye've goat the hoose tae yersel' and what dae ye dae, ye tidy up again don't ye? Mer ironin, light the fire, wash the dishes and the pots etc. etc. and then ye sit doon. And what happens . . . ye've just sat doon when the weans come up. 'Gonnae make us a cuppa tea and something tae eat' . . . What dae ye's want tae eat? . . . 'Och anything Ma' . . . D'ye want some o' that soup? . . . 'Naw' . . . A tomato sandwich? . . . 'Naw' . . . A couple o' boiled eggs? . . . 'Naw' . . . A piece 'n spam? . . . 'Naw' . . . Well what d'ye's want? . . . 'Och anything at all'. So ye make them something tae eat then ye sit doon and finally have a wee blaw . . . a very wee blaw . . . cause it's time tae go tae the steamie. Ye go tae the steamie, finish at nine o'clock and get the washin' hame. Ye sort it aw oot . . . and get it put by and then sometimes mebbe take stock of yer life. What are we? . . . skivvies . . . unpaid skivvies . . . in other words we are . . . used . . . but ye think tae yersel', well even if I am being used . . . I don't mind . . . cause I love my family and anyway it's New Year's Eve. I can relax and jist enjoy masel . . . and any minute noo the weans'll be in an ma friends'll be comin' roon wi' black bun, shortbread, dumplin's, a wee refreshment and I can forget aw ma worries even if it's jist for a night and the weans arrive and ye gie them shortbread, sultana cake, ginger wine and there is just one thing missin', the

> head of the family. The door bell goes, ye open the door, and what is staunin there, ready to make the evening complete . . . that's right . . . your husband, your better half . . . the man who was goin' to make you the happiest woman in the world and [*Gently.*] what does he look like . . . *that* [*At* ANDY.]
>
> DOLLY   Who were ye talkin' tae?
>
> MAGRIT   Masel.
>
> ANDY   So . . . z'a . . . wis sayin' girls . . . everything aw right doon here . . . know . . . cause . . . that's what I'm here fur.

What can you find in the passage which relates to Assessment Objectives 2i–5i? Remember that you need to provide evidence from the text for all your ideas. Here are some of the things you might think about:

AO2i: This is obviously from a play, but 'type' means more than genre. What type of play do you think it might be? What is the period? Think about the period that the play is set in, and the period when it was written – they might not be the same.

AO3: *Form* What is the effect of the stage directions? Who do you think Magrit's words are spoken to? This might make you speculate about the form of the whole play.

Language The language is obviously dialect, and the information given tells you it's Glasgow dialect. But there's a lot more to see. Think about the effect of the pronouns. Think about how humour is created, particularly with rhythm and repetition. Think about the tone – which words are obviously ironic? There's more, of course.

Structure Looking at the pronouns in the extract, and thinking about the form of the play might make you think about the structure, both of the passage here, and of the whole play. Look at the shape of Magrit's speech. How is it structured to finish the way it does?

AO4: Two obvious readings of the text are Marxist and feminist. Look for evidence of both. Is this really a feminist piece? Look carefully at the end of Magrit's speech.

AO5i: What different contexts can you find? Think about cultural, social and historical contexts, and the context of literary type and period.

In the examination

The most important thing to remember in the examination room is the importance of thinking and planning. You're full of knowledge, we hope, but it's easy to misuse it in the pressure of the exam, or at least not to use it effectively. Here's what you should do:

- Deconstruct the question. You know which Assessment Objectives are being targeted: look carefully for how they appear in the question, and at exactly what you're being asked to do. There's time allowed for thinking in the exam room. You've spent a long time reading your text, so you can afford the time to read the question several times, to make sure where the thrust of your response should be. There is a particular danger when you think you 'recognise' a question. You probably don't; it just looks a bit like something you've thought about, and it's all too easy to set off happily on the wrong track.

- Plan your response in detail. Structuring responses carefully, in a logical progression, will enable you to communicate your views clearly. Don't skip this; all too often candidates produce unstructured responses in the exam, in which the answer to the question doesn't start until halfway through.

- If you've planned clearly, you can spend your writing time following your plan, and choosing the best words and the best evidence to support what you say as you go.

Remember that in Module 3 you have to answer two questions, and you should aim to split your time equally between the two.

Glossary

Alienation a term used to describe an attempt by an author to prevent the audience or reader from identifying too closely with what is happening on the stage or in a text. The author reminds the audience/reader that what they see/read is a product of the writer's imagination. This could be applied to *Wise Children,* as we do not always believe what we read.

Allegory an extended metaphor, usually a narrative or description which works on two levels simultaneously. It usually carries a hidden moral meaning; for example, Rossetti's poem 'Up-Hill'.

Alliteration a sequence of two or more words beginning with the same letter placed close together, for example, from Duffy's 'Salome', 'clearing of clutter'.

Ambiguity occurs when it is possible to draw two or more meanings out of a literary work; for example, it is possible to read *Dr Faustus* as a warning about pride, or as a query about whether mankind may have such moral certainties as sin and redemption.

Appendices sections added on to the end of a book, often affecting the structure and meaning of the work, for example, as at the end of Ian McEwan's *Enduring Love.*

Archaic the use of a word, phrase or style which is deliberately old-fashioned and no longer in popular use; for example, Thomas Hardy's use of the word 'betides' in his poem 'Nature's Questioning'.

Association is the range of meanings which a word has acquired which have a personal significance to the user. *See* **connotation**.

Assonance the similarity of vowel sounds without actual rhyme, for example, 'dark hair, rather matted'. Here Duffy repeats the 'ar' sound to make contrasts in the line.

Chivalric code the rule of behaviour for knights in medieval times as defined in *The Romance of the Rose*, and satirised in Chaucer's *Miller's Tale.*

Colloquial informal language with familiar modes of speech as opposed to a formal use of language.

Conceit a far-fetched comparison in which you are forced to admit likeness between two things, whilst always being aware of the oddness of the comparison. The Metaphysical poets were famed for their use of conceits, such as Donne's image of the compasses to describe two lovers.

Connotation the extended significances of a word which are generally agreed; for example, purple is generally linked to royalty, mourning or Lent. *See* **association**.

Context in AS Literary Studies this is the fifth Assessment Objective. Contexts are the important facts, events or processes which have helped to shape literary works, for example, characteristics of contemporary styles.

Courtly love the code of behaviour a knight must follow in courting his lady in medieval times. This was defined in *The Romance of the Rose*, and satirised in Chaucer's *Miller's Tale*.

Cumulative a method of creating effects by the use of a series of repetitions.

Demotic popular, colloquial or vulgar language.

Detachment used when a writer adopts an impartial view of things.

Dialect is a form of language which is specific to a region or district, in which there is a particular idiom, pronunciation or vocabulary. For example, 'Scouse' is the Liverpudlian dialect.

Dialogue the part of literary works, particularly plays, written as conversation.

Diction is the vocabulary, the set of words a writer uses, for example, learned, homely, colloquial, archaic, etc.

Digression a part of a literary work in which the writer appears to have drifted away from the main subject.

Double entendre a phrase with two meanings, one of which is usually indecent, for example, Chaucer's use of 'eye' in *The Miller's Tale*.

Dramatic irony a situation in drama where the audience knows more than the characters on stage, for example, Marlowe's *Dr Faustus*.

Dramatic monologue a first-person narrative account in verse or prose.

End-stopped rhyme rhyming lines which contain a complete thought in each line.

Enjambment a term used in verse indicating that the sense of a line or couplet is carried over into the next line/couplet.

Epigraph a short inscription, often a quotation or poem, set at the beginning of a text. Epigraphs are usually related to the content that follows them, and may help set the tone.

Epilogue the concluding part of a literary work in which originally the actors addressed the audience; an author may address an epilogue at the end of a work to the reader.

Fabliau was originally a short tale in verse written in France, which was comic in style dealing with everyday life. In England, as in Chaucer's *Miller's Tale*, there was a comic, sexual element.

Figurative language language which contains figures of speech, for example, similes or metaphors.

Genre a specific type or style of literature or art.

Half-rhyme a type of verse in which the rhyme is not full, for example, rhyme created by assonance. *See* **assonance**.

Heroic couplet iambic pentameters rhyming in pairs, originally used by Chaucer and Shakespeare. *See* **iambic pentameter**.

Iambic pentameter a line of poetry with five weakly stressed syllables each followed by five strongly stressed syllables, for example Shakespeare's:

> ˘ ´ ˘ ´ ˘ ´ ˘ ´ ˘ ´
> When I do count the clock that tells the time.

Imagery images used by a writer of poetry or prose in which a picture or sense-impression is conveyed in words.

Interior monologue used when a writer conveys to the reader the thoughts of a character as they are being experienced.

Interlacing part of the medieval principle of construction in which ideas are woven together intricately.

Internal rhyme a line in poetry where there is rhyming inside the line, for example, 'shame' and 'name' in Rossetti's poem 'Noble Sisters'.

Irony present in writing of speech when the real meaning is concealed in words suggesting the opposite meaning, often as a means of criticism; for example, in the works of Geoffrey Chaucer, Thomas Hardy and Oscar Wilde.

Magic realism this form, which originated in Germany, and became very popular in South America, indicated a type of writing where the imaginary or fantastic was treated realistically. Later, as with Angela Carter, the term also suggested social comedy with a pleasing outcome.

Metaphor an implied or compressed comparison when one thing is said to take on the qualities of another, for example, Shakespeare's 'There's daggers in men's smiles'.

Metre the arrangement of stressed and unstressed syllables in a line of verse to produce a certain effect.

Miltonic literary writing in the style of Milton; when used about the sonnet form this indicates a sonnet composed of an octet followed by a sestet. *See* **Petrarchan**, **octet** and **sestet**.

Morality play medieval drama in verse in which abstractions such as Vice and Virtue were presented on stage.

Motif a dominant idea or image which reappears throughout a work, such as the use of the colour red in *The Handmaid's Tale*.

Objective the presentation of ideas uninfluenced by the writer's feelings or opinions.

Octet in the sonnet form the first eight-line section of a Miltonic sonnet.

Parody the use of another writer's form and style, sometimes to create satirical or comic effect.

Persona the adapting by a writer of the personality of someone else.

Personification the reference to an abstract idea in prose or poetry, as though it were a person, for example, Fanthorpe's 'The house fluttered' in 'Sirensong'.

Petrarchan the sonnet form originally created by Petrarch in the fourteenth century, and later used by Milton amongst others. *See* **Miltonic**.

Quatrain a stanza or sequence of four lines, sometimes with alternate rhymes.

Register a set of words used in specific circumstances or time period, for example, the different registers Golding uses in *The Spire*.

Satire literary work in which the aim is to amuse, criticise or correct by means of ridicule.

Sensuality related to the senses or sensations, usually with a sexual connotation rather than spiritual or intellectual.

Sensuous appealing to the senses but with no restriction to fleshly or sexual pleasure.

Sestet the second part of a Miltonic sonnet consisting of six lines, for example, the end of Rossetti's poem 'If Only'.

Shakespearean sonnet the sonnet form used by Shakespeare, consisting of three quatrains and a final summative couplet, or two rhymed lines.

Sibilance a series of words with a hissing sound such as 's' and 'sh'.

Simile a figure of speech using 'as' or 'like' in which there is a comparison used for clarity or vividness, for example, Carter's 'Brown as a quail' in *Wise Children*.

Stanza another name for a verse in a poem, with a set number of rhymes. The word comes from the Italian 'little room', as successive stanzas in a poem were seen to be like the rooms in a house, separate, but each leading out of one another.

Stream of consciousness a literary style which follows, without obvious external structuring, the internal successive thought processes of a character.

Subjective writing which aims to promote a personal point of view, and which is therefore not impartial.

Surrealism writing in which things are presented as though perceived in a dream or in the subconscious mind, and not in a way which would seem to be realistic in an everyday way. An example is the account of Perry's magic tricks in *Wise Children*.

Symbolism a literary style originated in France in the nineteenth century in which the writer tries to create impressions rather than to describe things accurately.

Syntax the grammatical arrangement of words in writing or speech.

Theology the science or study of religion concerned with the knowledge of God, evident in Christina Rossetti's Christian beliefs.